THE SCRIPTURE
OF TRUTH

THE SCRIPTURE OF TRUTH

George S. Syme
Charlotte U. Syme

THE SCRIPTURE OF TRUTH: A LAYMAN'S GUIDE TO
UNDERSTANDING HOW THE BIBLE IS INSPIRED

Copyright © 1983 by Mott Media, Inc.

All rights reserved. No portion of this book may be reproduced without permission from the publisher except by a reviewer who may quote brief passages in connection with a review. For information address Mott Media, Inc., 1000 East Huron Street, Milford, Michigan, 48042.

Leonard George Goss, Editor

Copyedited by Leonard George Goss and Ruth Schenk
Cover designed by Joe Ragont Studios, Inc.
Typeset by Frieda Bohn and Joyce Bohn
Printed by BookCrafters

Manufactured in the United States of America

ISBN 0-88062-019-6

In appreciation to
the Fellowship Bible Class
of
Grace Bible Church
Souderton, PA
who for over 20 years have patiently allowed George
to practice on them the materials that have evolved into
this book and other studies.

CONTENTS

	Foreword by Norman L. Geisler	ix
	Preface	xi
1	Why Do We Need A Doctrine Of Scripture?	1
2	What Does Scripture Say About Itself?	9
3	Can We Test The Bible's Claims?	19
4	How Do Some Attempt To Undermine The Trustworthiness Of Scripture?	29
5	How Do We Know What Books Are Scripture? (Old Testament Canon)	39
6	How Do We Know What Books Are Scripture? (New Testament Canon)	49
7	How Has God Preserved His Word?	63
8	Do We Really Have The Scripture That God Inspired?	71
9	How Has The Bible Come Into English?	83
10	Which Version Should I Use?	91
11	How Can I Get More Out Of Bible Study?	101
12	What Is My Responsibility To An Infallible Bible?	113

Foreword

The psalmist said, "If the foundation be destroyed what shall the righteous do" (Psa. 11:3). Since the turn of the century, and before, Christians have considered certain teachings foundational or fundamental to their faith. Among these several have stood out: 1) The inspiration and inerrancy of Scripture, 2) the Virgin Birth of Christ, 3) the deity of Christ, 4) His substitutionary atonement, 5) Christ's bodily resurrection, and 6) His Second Coming. Now of these fundamentals of the faith the last five are all based on the first one—an inspired Bible. Hence, it can be truly said that the inspiration of Scripture is the fundamental of the fundamentals. In view of this we may pose a fundamental question: if the fundamental of the fundamentals is not fundamental, then what is fundamental? The answer is: fundamentally nothing!

It is very important that the lay Christian understands the basis on which his faith rests. *The Scripture of Truth* is a helpful, biblical, and practical attempt to fill this need. Jesus said, "the Scripture cannot be broken" (John 10:35). In these pages the lay reader will find ample grounds for encouragement in his belief in this infallible Word of which Jesus spoke.

Many voices in our day claim that the Bible has errors; this they insist is the truth. In contrast to this claim the authors of this book affirm with the apostle Paul, "Let God be true but every man a liar" (Rom. 3:4). The following pages will assist the careful reader to appreciate more fully the significance of our Lord's pronouncement, "Verily I say unto you, Till heaven and earth pass, one jot or one tittle shall in no wise pass from the law, till all be fulfilled" (Matt. 5:18).

This book, along with those generated by the International Council on Biblical Inerrancy, is destined to contribute to the increased understanding of the men and women in the pew whose very lives depend on a sure word from God. For, as the apostle declares, "if the trumpet gives an uncertain sound, who shall prepare himself to the battle" (I Cor. 14:8)?

                                        Norman L. Geisler
                                        Dallas Theological Seminary

PREFACE

Martin Luther said that if you do not meet the devil at the point where he is attacking, you are not really fighting for the truth. In our day, one frequent point of attack is against the idea of the inerrancy of the Scriptures. Not too long ago inerrancy was one of the basic tenets of conservative Christianity, held by virtually everyone who called themselves evangelical. Jesus said, "Thy Word is truth" (John 17:17); for those who believed Him, that settled the matter. In recent years, however, this teaching has been redefined and complicated by theologians who claim to accept every doctrine that is fundamental to our Christian faith.

This book is not intended to be either a theological treatise on the doctrine of Scripture, or a specialists' presentation of what the term means. Excellent scholarly works are available on these subjects. This book is for the layman in the pew who is confused at hearing those he trusts as Christian leaders state that the Bible is only "religiously" true, or that it is inerrant only when it discusses doctrines and duties. Or, they remind us that we do not possess the original manuscripts of the Bible writers. Thus it becomes necessary to examine why the truth of all Scripture cannot be dismissed by such reasoning. We hope we have presented in plain language the reasons why we can trust our Bible totally, and explained clearly the basis for our assurance that the Scriptures we possess are substantially identical with the original writings. Our contents have been tested in real teaching situations—both in Sunday school and in laymen's Bible class groups.

"Be ready always to give . . . a reason for the hope that is within you," Peter admonished his flock (1 Peter 3:15). We send this book out with the prayer that some who trust in and live by the Book of our faith will be better prepared to explain to others why they can accept it as the Scripture of truth. We further trust that some who have wavered or been confused by the pronouncements of teachers in high places will be re-established on the firm foundation of the Word of God—the Scripture of Truth.

George S. Syme
Charlotte U. Syme

Chapter 1

Why Do We Need A Doctrine Of Scripture?

An old story that frequently turns up in collections of sermon illustrations tells of a woman who went to her liberal pastor and showed him her Bible. On page after page the text had been blacked out until the blocks of blackness far exceeded the passages of print. When the minister asked her why she had done it she replied, "Every time you said that something in the Bible was not to be taken literally, or was not for us, or was in error as to the facts, I blacked it out. Now that so little is left I want to know if I have anything on which to base my faith."

Such is the inevitable quandary of anyone who attempts to divide the Bible into those utterances which are inspired of God and inerrant, and those that are only incidentally included and contain the fallacies common to men of their time.

Many Christians find doctrine a scary word. They relate it to ivory-tower theologians and scholarly seminaries where six-syllable vocabularies are sprinkled with German expressions. But the root of the word is merely "teaching" or "instruction." The doctrine of any branch of knowledge is its basic and authoritative teachings. What we believe concerning the Scripture is our doctrine of Scripture.

The Bible: Basis of Knowledge

The only basic source of Christian doctrine is the Bible.

Whenever there is a question concerning what to believe about the nature of God or the deity of Christ or the sinfulness of man or the culmination of history, or any other matter included in the body of Christian teaching, the answer must ultimately stem from the Bible. Even if we take our questions to a minister, teacher or recognized scholar, we must confirm the validity of their replies by checking them against the authority of "what saith the Scripture" in order to evaluate their answers or opinions.

It follows, therefore, that the doctrine of Scripture is basic to all other doctrines (God, Christ, the Holy Spirit, man, sin, salvation, the church, eschatology, etc.). If the Bible is absolutely reliable, all the rest stands on a firm foundation. If, however, it contains error, how are we to know what we can trust and what we cannot? God's Word is not a tray of canapes from which to choose only those texts that appeal to us. Such an attitude makes individual judgment the ultimate authority and robs us of any foundation for assurance in our faith. Without such assurance, we are of all men most miserable.

Whether or not we are consciously aware of it, we each have a doctrine of Scripture. We may express it in some such words as, "I believe such and such because the Bible says it," or, "I am behaving in this manner because the Bible commands it." But if asked why it is right to believe and obey the Bible so implicitly, can we answer? When people who claim to be evangelical believers, born again by the blood of Christ, tell us that a distinction must be made between the "religious" and "incidental" statements in the Bible, how can we know they are wrong? If they say, "Only the original writings are inerrant and we do not possess those," how are we to reply? Can you give a "reason for the hope that is in you?"[1]

Basis of our knowledge of God. One of the basic texts on which our doctrine of Scripture is built is 2 Peter 1:16-21. In order to see more fully the import of what Peter is saying, we must look at its context. How to discern true knowledge of God from false teaching is the basic subject of the three chapters

Why Do We Need A Doctrine Of Scripture?

which comprise the epistle. Peter begins by reminding us in chapter 1 that our faith is a gift of God, provided through the righteousness of our Saviour (v. 1). He speaks of the blessings that should mark our lives because of our faith—grace and peace (v. 2) and assurance (v. 10). This assurance is available to us because of our knowledge of God and of Christ and of what they have done for us. He expects that we have a knowledge of His promises (v. 4) and that our faith will be increased by that knowledge (v. 5). It is as we increase our knowledge of Christ that we increase our fruitfulness as His people (v.8).

Peter wants his readers to know how they can be sure that the gospel he has taught them really is true knowledge and not one of the false teachings which have already begun to creep into the church. He emphasizes that he is not following "cunningly devised fables" (vv. 16-18 - a clear reference to pagan mythology) such as the pagans do, because he himself was an eyewitness to the majestic glory of Christ revealed on the Mount of Transfiguration where he heard the voice of God attesting that this was indeed His beloved Son. At this point (v. 19) Peter puts himself on a par with the prophets of the Old Testament as one who is speaking the revelation of God. He is as prophetic as they and is in harmony with the Scripture that had already been written. That Scripture is absolutely sure because it is not the words of men recording their thoughts about God, but is the very Word of God to men (vv. 20-21). Here it is in contrast to the "fables" of the Greeks. These verses comprise one of the definitive passages concerning the testimony of the Bible to itself.

Because false teachers are already infiltrating the church, Peter is concerned lest some of his converts go astray after he is no longer around to keep them straight (2 Peter 1:13-15). Therefore, in chapter 2, he discusses how to discern between what is taught by true and false prophets. He proposes two tests that will expose a false teacher: 1) their attitude toward Christ (2 Peter 2:1), and 2) their manner of life (2 Peter 2:2). These two tests are still basic in dealing with seducing teachers and false cults today. Even those cults that claim to be biblically based reveal the falsity of their claims if they downgrade the person of Christ and/or lead personal lives contrary to what the Scripture commands.

Peter illustrates his point by mentioning the angels that sinned (2 Peter 2:4), the old world in the days of Noah (2 Peter 2:5), Sodom and Gomorrah (2 Peter 2:6), Lot (2 Peter 2:7-9), Balaam (2 Peter 2:15-16). He implies that these people and events are matters of sober history that we can rely on for knowledge of the ways of God and His dealings with men as well as for the marks of true and false teachers. His illustrations are particularly significant in the light of recent attacks on the authority and trustworthiness of Scripture, and especially of the historical accuracy of the Pentateuch, since all the events he mentions come from those first five books.[2]

In chapter 3, Peter takes up one specific and widespread false teaching. It concerns the culmination of history as taught in Scripture. In order to avoid falling for false teaching on this subject, he says, we must be mindful of the words which were spoken before by the holy prophets, and of the commandment of us the apostles of the Lord and Saviour" (2 Peter 3:2). In other words, the Old Testament (the prophets) and the New Testament (the apostles) are equally authoritative and together make up the whole body of Scripture. Then, lest anyone quibble that "us the apostles" might exclude the writings of Paul from the canon of Scripture, the Holy Spirit led Peter to pen verses 15 and 16, thereby putting the stamp of Scriptural authority on the entire Bible.

The significant point of 2 Peter as it relates to the doctrine of Scripture is that Peter has put the writings of the apostles on an equal footing with the Old Testament prophets. To have true knowledge, therefore, we must base our faith on the whole message of the prophets and apostles, and not on the cunningly devised fables of men.

Basis of our knowledge of ourselves. Not only would our knowledge of God be very rudimentary apart from the revelation of

Why Do We Need A Doctrine of Scripture?

Himself in Scripture, but even our knowledge of ourselves would be most limited. Observation may inform us that man is evil (although modern psychologists have developed alternate positions even on that), but only the Scripture tells us why.[3] It is also Scripture that teaches us we cannot perfect ourselves. Our sinfulness is incurable apart from the righteousness of God.[4]

It is ignorance and deliberate rejection of Scripture that has so warped our legal and sociological dealings. Until recent times western society has been based on biblical concepts of right and wrong, with the Ten Commandments in a prominent position. Only in our century have men turned from these biblical absolutes to the relativity of sociological expedients for evaluating man's evil tendencies and seeking solutions to his problems. The Ten Commandments themselves can be displayed on schoolroom walls only if the courts allow it! The result is the uncertainty of today's legal profession. No longer are there any absolutes. What is right and wrong is no longer a matter of divine authority, but of sociological fads. Our times have become known as the post-Christian era. We need a strong doctrine of Scripture, not only for a true knowledge about God and about ourselves as individuals, but also in order to have a stable society.

The Bible: Written for Our Profit

Peter's second epistle was written very near the end of his life. Knowing it was probably his last communication to his readers, he considered the doctrine of Scripture to be the most important subject he could stress as his final word to them. Likewise, 2 Timothy was Paul's last epistle, written very shortly before his execution, and he, too, majors on the importance of the Scripture. In it he exhorts his disciple, Timothy, to study it (2 Timothy 2:15), preach it (2 Timothy 2:16), and live by it (2 Timothy 3:17).

Like 2 Peter, this epistle also contains a passage that is definitive for any discussion of the doctrine of Scripture. After reminding Timothy that the Scripture is his foundation for knowledge—particularly for the knowledge of salvation (2 Timothy 3:15), he suggests the many ways in which it is still profitable. In other words, the Scripture is not given merely that we might have a body of knowledge concerning salvation, and perhaps to satisfy our intellectual questionings, but that we might have a body of usable knowledge—first, in respect to right doctrine (this is how we become "wise unto salvation"), and then that our lives might be corrected and instructed and directed into maturity and good works. Paul's doctrine of Scripture is two pronged: it is God-given and it is intended for our profit.

Paul believed in plenary inspiration—that the Scripture originated entirely with God. What he literally says in the Greek is, "Every Scripture is God-breathed;" that is, God is its source.[5]

"We shall know them by their fruits."[6] God's Word can be known by what it produces—mature believers who are well-equipped for Christian service. The Scripture is both God-breathed and profitable. It is profitable because it is God-breathed. Not only is it our source of knowledge of God and of ourselves, but it is our source of wisdom—the ability to rightly use knowledge. Because Timothy had knowledge of the Scripture, he had the necessary means to become a fully equipped ("throughly furnished") and mature ("perfect") Christian. There is no other source for this knowledge and wisdom except the Scripture. This is why it is vital that we be absolutely assured of its complete trustworthiness in every part. It is not enough to say it is infallible in questions of faith and practice, for who are we to sit in judgment on any of it by saying, "this passage has nothing to do with faith and practice and thus need not necessarily be considered infallible." It is just as much God-breathed and profitable when it appears to be discussing only history, geography, science or other earthly subjects, as when it is obviously discussing belief and behavior. Jesus said, "If I have told you earthly things and ye believe not, how will ye believe if I tell you heavenly things?"[7] It is the Scripture which

Why Do We Need A Doctrine of Scripture? 7

is to sit in judgment on us, and that includes our understanding of "earthly things."

For all these reasons it is vital that we not only have a doctrine of Scripture, but that we know why we hold the doctrine that we do rather than the contrary arguments of men—even of some men who also call themselves Christians.

SUMMARY

An understanding of the Biblical doctrine of Scripture is vital in our day when even professing Christians seek to do away with biblical inerrancy by making a division between its "religious" and its "incidental" statements. No man is qualified to make this distinction.

Because there is no absolute knowledge apart from a revelation from God, we can neither know Him nor His requirements of us, nor can we understand ourselves and our interrelationships, apart from His Word. The apostle Peter demonstrated in his second epistle that the Scripture is the necessary bedrock on which to build our knowledge of truth and to distinguish between true and false teachers. Paul, in writing to Timothy, insisted on the priority of Scripture both for Christian birth and Christian maturity.

Our attitude toward Scripture determines our attitude toward all else that pertains to our Christian belief and behavior. It is essential that we know for certain that God has given us an absolutely inerrant and perfect revelation.

FOOTNOTES

[1] 1 Peter 3:15
[2] Gen. 6—8; 19; Num. 22—24
[3] Gen. 3
[4] Rom. 1—5
[5] There has been considerable discussion among theologians as to whether this passage should not instead be translated "every inspired Scripture," thus leaving open how much of the Bible is included. The old ASV did this, but the New American Standard Bible does not follow its predecessor. Even more liberal translations as the RSV, Moffatt and Weymouth agree with the more

traditional translation of the King James. Only the NEB follows the ASV. A. T. Robertson, a leading Greek scholar, says the traditional way is the more natural usage of the Greek, although the other translation is linguistically possible (*Word Pictures in the New Testament*, IV, p. 627). Furthermore, the context shows that the inspired Scripture to which Paul referred was that which Timothy had been taught as a child—the Old Testament.

[6]Matt. 7:16
[7]John 3:12

Chapter 2

What Does Scripture Say About Itself?

Internal Evidence

Critics of the inspiration of Scripture accuse Christians of using a "circular argument" when insisting that the Bible is the inspired Word of God and then quoting Scripture to support the claim. The complaint is unfounded. Where would be a better place to begin such a demonstration than in the words of the Bible itself? If it made no such claim, we would have no need to make one for it. Since it does claim to be God's infallible Word, we must pay heed and those who would deny it must show the claim to be unfounded. As in a court of law one is permitted to testify in his own behalf, so the Bible's own testimony should be permitted here. It is the proper starting point for developing a doctrine of Scripture. That which we learn about the divine origin of Scripture from its own testimony we call the "internal evidence" of inspiration.

Claims of Inspiration in the Old Testament

It is impossible to abolish the Old Testament's claim to be a revelation from God by explaining away any particular text. The teaching is too tightly woven throughout all the Old Testament.

It all began with Moses. The Old Testament's claim to be God-given traces back to Moses at the burning bush. When given his assignment to lead Israel out of Egypt, he complained, "They will not believe me, nor hearken unto my voice" (Exodus 4:1). So the Lord gave three signs to prove that Moses was His spokesman. Israel accepted them, but Pharaoh refused to and the ten plagues followed. In the final miracle, the army of Pharaoh was overwhelmed in the sea. Each of these events occurred as Moses had forewarned according to the command of God.[1]

Although Israel had many murmurings and backslidings in the wilderness—and even challenged Moses' authority—time and again they received clear evidence that Moses talked with God and that when he spoke, he spoke the words of God. When he collected these messages into the five books we call the Pentateuch[2], there were living eyewitnesses who knew that when "Moses wrote all the words of the LORD" (Exodus 24:4), he was really giving God's own words to Israel.

Although Exodus 24:4 is the most specific claim in the Pentateuch, there are numerous other places where we read: "And the LORD said," "and the LORD spoke," etc., followed by statements in the first person. If you use the American Standard Version you will find not "LORD" but "Jehovah," which is the most literal translation. It is important to realize that whenever the King James Version has LORD or GOD in small capitals, the Hebrew text has the four letters that stand for the name of the God of Israel—Jehovah (or Yahweh).[3]

These claims that Moses was writing God's words and law are climaxed in Deuteronomy 31:24-26. "And it came to pass, when Moses had made an end of writing the words of this law in a book, until they were finished, That Moses commanded the Levites, which bare the ark of the covenant of the LORD, saying, Take this book of the law, and put it in the side of the ark of the covenant of the LORD your God, that it may be there for a witness against thee."

There are three important points in this text that are relevant to our contention that the Pentateuch claims to be the Word of God. 1. The law (Torah) is called "the covenant of the

What Does Scripture Say About Itself?

LORD." 2. Moses is credited with its authorship. 3. It was so important—so sacred—that it was to occupy a place in the ark of the covenant beside the pot of manna, Aaron's rod that budded, and the tables of stone on which were written the Ten Commandments.[4] To this day the receptacle in a synagogue where the Scripture is kept is called the ark.

A continuing revelation in Old Testament times. There is good reason why "there arose not a prophet since in Israel like unto Moses, whom the LORD knew face to face" (Deuteronomy 34:10). From the time Moses laid down his pen, Israel had God's revelation in written, permanent form. The Word begun in the books of Moses would be expanded, explained and built upon by later prophets, but it would not be altered, abrogated or contradicted. Israel now had an absolute authority against which to judge their beliefs, their behavior, and the claims anyone else might make to have a word from God.

Notice the instructions the Lord gave to Joshua, Moses' successor. Joshua's business was to fulfill his mission according "as I said unto Moses" (Joshua 1:3), "to observe to do according to all the law which Moses my servant commanded thee, Turn not from it to the right hand or to the left, that thou mayest prosper wherever thou goest. This book of the law shall not depart out of thy mouth; but thou shalt meditate therein day and night, that thou mayest observe to do according to all that is written therein" (Joshua 1:7-8).

For the first time in human history, man was commanded to order his life according to a book. Clearly, Joshua had the completed Torah and it formed the basis of Scripture for all succeeding generations. It was recognized from the time of its production as God's Word.

Not only Joshua, but all future leaders, including kings, were commanded to be subject to the precepts of the Book. In anticipation of a monarchy, Moses had given instructions for the conduct of a king. The most important of these was that he was to make his own written copy of the Torah and "read therein all the days of his life" (Deuteronomy 17:18-20). We know from many of the Psalms how much David delighted in the Word of God.[5] When he turned the kingdom over to his son Solomon, he instructed him in words that remind us of God's instruction to Joshua: "Be thou strong, therefore, and show thyself a man, and keep the charge of the LORD thy God, to walk in his ways, to keep his statutes, and his commandments and his ordinances and his testimonies, as it is written in the law of Moses" (1 Kings 2:3).

Throughout the history of the kingdom we find that revival came whenever the nation returned to God's Word. And after the people returned from their Babylonian captivity, they based their new life on the Torah and its precepts, which Ezra and the nation regarded as God's Word "which the LORD had commanded to Israel (Nehemiah 8:1, 8, 14).

However, God's revelation was not completed with the books of Moses. In them He made provision for recognition of a continuing revelation. In Deuteronomy 18, He promised that there would arise other prophets. They would be recognized by the fact that what they foretold would come to pass. "When a prophet speaketh in the name of the LORD, if the thing follow not nor come to pass, that is the thing which the LORD hath not spoken but the prophet hath spoken it presumptuously; thou shalt not be afraid of him" (Deuteronomy 18:22).

In other words, the messages of the Old Testament prophets were validated by the fact that their prophecies were fulfilled. Yet even in the face of such exacting conditions, there arose false prophets claiming to speak for God. An example of this is in 1 Kings 22:5-28 where one named Zedekiah with about four hundred associates sought to flatter King Ahab with predictions of victory while Micaiah, one lone man of God, steadfastly spoke the unpopular truth. Another such imposter accused Jeremiah of being a lying prophet. Jeremiah declared that the accuser would die within the year and he did (Jeremiah 28).

A second test for judging a false prophet was that if his teaching conflicted with God's already revealed Word, he was to be rejected even if he could produce signs and wonders. He

What Does Scripture Say About Itself?

was to be "put to death because he hath spoken to turn you away from the LORD your God" (Deuteronomy 13:1-5). Thus in Old Testament times did God provide for a continuing revelation, giving His people two tests by which they could ascertain whether a new message was in fact His Word.

To sum up: the Old Testament claims 3808 times[7] to be giving the words of God, and the prophets were accepted only when their messages were divinely validated.

Claims in the New Testament

The writer of Hebrews tells us that Jesus Christ is God's last word to man—His final and complete revelation.[8] Yet he also insists that God spoke as truly—though not as finally—in the prophets that preceded Christ. Since our Lord is God's last word, it is important to know that He personally validated both the Old Testament writings and those that would be produced concerning Himself.

Claims concerning the Old Testament. Long before the birth of Christ, the Old Testament was complete just as we have it today. It had already taken on the arrangement of books that it still has in the Hebrew Bible (see fig. 1), and it was unquestioningly accepted as the Word of God. It is repeatedly quoted as Scripture (that is, as God's revelation) in the New Testament as well as in other ancient Jewish writings, such as those found among the Dead Sea scrolls. Many times it is simply called "the law" (Torah), or "the law and the prophets." There are, however, two occasions which reveal that the Old Testament Scriptures were already arranged in the order they still have in today's Hebrew Bible.

1. Luke 24:44: "And he said unto them, These are the words which I spake unto you, while I was yet with you, that all things must be fulfilled, which were written in the law of Moses, and in the prophets, and in the psalms, concerning me."

Clearly these words refer to the threefold division of the Hebrew Scripture shown in figure 1. The Torah of Moses and the prophets are obviously the first and second division. The word *psalms* requires some explanation. In the ancient world books were usually called by their first word: e.g., Genesis was named *Beresheth* (meaning "in the beginning"). In an extension of this, collections were often titled by their initial work. We have the same practice today in books of short stories or essays titled the same as the first story. The third division of the Hebrew arrangement begins with the Books of Psalms. Thus, by citing Psalms, our Lord was referring not only to the messianic Psalms but to the many other references to Himself contained in Psalms through Chronicles. This is made clear in the two references that follow.

2. Matthew 23:35; Luke 11:51. Both these verses make sense only if understood to refer to the Hebrew order of Scripture. Abel, of course was the first to be slain.[9] But Zechariah was certainly not the last prophet to die for his faith. However, in the Hebrew order of Scripture, Chronicles is the last book of the Old Testament, and Zechariah is the last martyr described therein.[10] Thus "Abel to Zechariah" is comparable to our expression "from Genesis to Revelation" when we refer to the whole Bible.

To these examples may be added numerous Old Testament quotations throughout the New Testament as well as the important verses in 2 Timothy and 2 Peter that we studied in chapter 1.[11] Thus the apostles followed the teaching of Christ who clearly accepted the Old Testament Scriptures as God's Word, saying that He had not come to destroy the law but to fulfill it (Matthew 5:17) and that God's Word "cannot be broken" (John 10:35). Time and again He appealed to it to justify His words and His actions.

Claims of the New Testament concerning itself. Just before the crucifixion, Jesus placed His stamp of authority on the yet-to-be-written New Testament by promising to send the Holy Spirit who would guide His apostles "into all truth" and would show them "things to come." (John 16:13). Peter alludes to this promise in 1 Peter 1:12.

The apostolic authority of Paul's writings cannot be set

aside any more than can that of Peter or John. He claims in Galatians 1:12 to have been taught of the Lord. In 1 Thessalonians, commonly regarded as his earliest epistle and possibly the earliest New Testament writing, he comments: "When ye received the word of God which ye heard of us, ye received it not as the word of men but as it is in truth, the word of God, which effectually worketh also in you that believe" (1 Thessalonians 2:13). He commanded the Corinthians to test the claims and credentials of every teacher who came among them by letting them "acknowledge that the things that I write unto you are the commands of the Lord" (1 Corinthians 14:37). And all his teaching was based solidly on the Old Testament. Nor are we dependent on Paul's own testimony alone for his claims to be writing God's Word; we saw in chapter 1 how Peter also validated Paul's authority.[12]

Charles Wesley has been quoted as saying that the Bible could not have its source in good men or angels because they would become liars by saying that their words were the words of God; nor could it have been written by bad men or devils because it exposes and condemns them. It must be all that it claims—the very Word of God, having its source in Him and revealed by inspiration to His chosen prophets and apostles. We have seen how this claim is inextricably imbedded in the entire Scripture.

SUMMARY

Our major reason for insisting that the Bible is God's inerrant Word and not a mere human writing is that Scripture itself, from beginning to end, makes this claim, and our Lord who is God's final revelation endorsed it. Moses and all his successors were conscious of being the spokesmen of Jehovah, and their claims were validated by the fact that their prophecies were fulfilled. The New Testament apostles were also conscious of their divine commission as the Holy Spirit directed them.

These claims of the Scripture itself from its own pages are called the internal evidence of the divine inspiration of the Bible.

FOOTNOTES

[1] Exod. 8-14.

[2] Pentateuch comes from the Greek, meaning five tools or implements. The Hebrew word for the five books is *Torah*, or Law. Pentateuch, Torah, Law, Books of Moses, are all synonyms for the first five books of the Bible.

[3] Later versions returned to the use of LORD (Hebrew: *Adonai*) for reasons of style and in keeping with the Greek texts. The Hebrews never pronounced the sacred name of God and, in reading aloud, always substituted *Adonai* wherever the name Jehovah occurred.

[4] Exod. 16:33, 34; 25:16; 40:20; Num. 17:10; Heb. 9:4.

[5] Psalms 19 and 119 are only two of the better known places.

[6] All these words are used throughout the Bible as synonyms for the Word of God.

[7] According to Dr. William Evans, *The Great Doctrines of the Bible* (Chicago: Moody Press, 1974), p. 203.

[8] Heb. 1:1, 2.

[9] Gen. 4.

[10] 2 Chron. 24:20-22.

[11] 2 Tim. 3:16; 2 Peter 1:19-21.

[12] 2 Peter 3:15, 16.

THE ARRANGEMENT OF OLD TESTAMENT BOOKS IN HEBREW AND GREEK BIBLES

The Hebrew Scriptures	The Greek Septuagint (LXX) (followed in Latin and English Bibles)
The Law (Torah)—5 books	The Law (Pentateuch)—5 books
Genesis	Genesis
Exodus	Exodus
Leviticus	Leviticus
Numbers	Numbers
Deuteronomy	Deuteronomy
The Prophets (Nebhiim)—8 books	History—12 books
Former Prophets	Joshua
Joshua	Judges
Judges	Ruth
Samuel	1 Samuel
Kings	2 Samuel

What Does Scripture Say About Itself?

Latter Prophets	1 Kings
Isaiah	2 Kings
Jeremiah	1 Chronicles
Ezekiel	2 Chronicles
The Twelve (1 book)	Ezra
Hosea	Nehemiah
Joel	Esther
Amos	Poetry—5 books
Obadiah	Job
Jonah	Psalms
Micah	Proverbs
Nahum	Ecclesiastes
Habakkuk	Song of Solomon
Zephaniah	Prophets—17 books
Haggai	Major:
Zechariah	Isaiah
Malachi	Jeremiah
The Writings (Kethubhim)—11 books	Lamentations
Poetical Books	Ezekiel
Psalms	Daniel
Proverbs	Minor:
Job	Hosea
The Five Rolls (Megilloth)	Joel
Song of Songs	Amos
Ruth	Obadiah
Lamentations	Jonah
Esther	Micah
Ecclesiastes	Nahum
Historical Books	Habakkuk
Daniel	Zephaniah
Ezra-Nehemiah	Haggai
Chronicles	Zechariah
	Malachi
Total: 24 books	Total: 39 books

Fig. 1

Chapter 3

Can We Test The Bible's Claims?

External Evidence

As Christians we recognize that the Scripture's own claims to be God's direct revelation to man are sufficient base for our belief and behavior. We accept it because our Lord, who is God's final and complete revelation, has put His stamp of authority upon it. "God has spoken," the author of Hebrews tells us, through His prophets, but finally and completely through His Son.[1] These internal evidences of the Bible's witness to itself were discussed in chapter 2.

Having said this, we recognize that many who are potential converts have grown up hearing from their teachers, and even from some ministers, that the Bible is no more directly inspired than are the best of human writings. It is often possible to bring such people closer to the decisive step of faith if we can defend our doctrine of Scripture by appeals to reason and to objective evidences. Our justification for this approach comes from Peter who commanded that we "be ready always to give an answer to every man that asketh you a reason of the hope that is in you" (1 Peter 3:15). Paul also gave us an example of such reasoning when he buttressed his message to the philosophers of Athens by appealing to the creation and to the works of the Greek poets.[2] We call these arguments external evidences to distinguish them from the internal evidences that are based on what the Scripture says about itself. External evidences may be divided into two types: evidence based on reason, and evidence based on historical fact.

Evidence Based on Reason

"Come now, and let us reason together, saith the LORD" (Isaiah 1:18). The God who created us made us creatures with mental faculties able to reason, and He invites us to use our reason. But notice, He invites us to use it with Him: "Let us reason together." When we try to reason rebelliously and in defiance of Him, the result is unreasonable and chaotic thinking. Rightly used, reason leads to knowledge of Him and understanding of His Word.

Arguments from the character of God. Since God made us in His image,[3] we can understand some things about God because the finite version of many of His characteristics appears in us. We can expect Him to be a communicating God because we ourselves are communicators. Nor are we satisfied with communication on the animal level that is limited to the necessary warnings, mating call, etc. for survival. Man wants to share himself—his thoughts, his dreams, his very soul, with others capable of understanding and sharing in turn. Even Adam recognized this need before the Lord gave him Eve.[4] Does it not appear then that the God in whose image we are created is a communicating God and that He equipped us with that elaborate means of communication—language—in order that we might be prepared to receive communication from Him?

Of all means of communication, writing is the most advanced, and among civilized men it is considered the most trustworthy (e.g., "Will you put that in writing?"). A written statement of a man's words is accepted as more reliable than his or his hearers' memory of what he said. Then should we be surprised that the most important communication we can receive—the revelation of God and His will—should be in the form of a written record?

Furthermore, we cannot have communication with God unless

Can We Test The Bible's Claims?

He chooses to invade our world, because the five senses through which we receive communication cannot touch God nor imprison Him in a test tube. With the coming of sin our spiritual sense that could be in contact with God died. He must remain forever unknowable unless He chooses to reveal Himself in our space-time environment. To quote Thiessen: "Man being what he is and God being what He is, we may possibly expect a revelation from God and also an embodiment of such parts of that revelation as are needed to supply a reliable and infallible source of theological truth."[5]

Hence it is evident that for man to have any true theology, God would have to convey to him some body of rules, instructions, explanations or other lessons that would embody His will. Writing such as the Bible would be the result.

Argument from the character of the Bible. Honest reason should convince us that the nature of the Bible itself shows that it cannot be a mere human document. At least four evidences substantiate this.

1. Its indestructibility. Most books have a very short life. Few survive their generation, and those that last for centuries are rare indeed. There was an abundance of literature in ancient times. "Of making of books there is no end," said the preacher.[6] Yet only a small fraction has come down to us, and most of that in incomplete and hopelessly corrupt form. But the text of the Bible has survived with remarkable completeness and accuracy.

Furthermore, it has survived countless persecutions and determined efforts to destroy it from as early as the time of Jeremiah.[7] Since then Roman emperors, Moslem hordes, Communists and Nazis—even leaders of the church—have tried to suppress and destroy the Bible. Not only has it survived, it has been translated into more languages than any other writing. Voltaire once stated that in one hundred years Christianity would be a forgotten faith and the Bible a historical curiosity. Yet, in far less time than that, his house had become the headquarters of the Geneva Bible Society and the printing presses that produced his works were helping to turn out Bibles for the ends of the earth.

2. Its character. Besides its indestructibility, consider its contents. It begins with an account of creation that W. F. Albright called "unique to ancient literature," adding "that it may be seriously doubted whether science has yet caught up with the biblical story."[8]

Its descriptions of a holy God and sinful men are such that man neither could nor would produce it. The gods conceived in the minds of men—such as those of the ancient Babylonians, Canaanites, Greeks and Romans—are only larger-than-life men and women with human virtues and vices on a heroic scale. They have more in common with Superman, Batman and the Bionic Woman than they do with true deity. Man cannot from his own fallen imagination conceive a person of infinite holiness.

3. Its unity. Consider also the unity of the Bible. Although written by over forty different authors over a period of more than 1600 years, it is in every sense of the work, one Book. It maintains a consistent picture of God's character, and a consistent and unequalled moral standard for man. From beginning to end it tells one story. Beginning with creation, through man's fall, God's arrangement for his salvation, and the consummation of history, it is the story of God's purpose for man and the fulfillment of that purpose. It centers on one Person—Jesus Christ, who is the focus of all Scripture.

4. Its influence. Consider finally the influence of the Bible. No other writing, not even those claimed by other religions to be sacred, can approach the influence Scripture has had on civilization. It is impossible to tabulate its mark on the arts, architecture, literature, government, law, morality, human social relationships and character. It has had universal appeal and applicability from the great cities of western civilization to the most remote jungles. Some of our greatest thinkers, even some who were not personally Christians, have credited the rise of science and technololgy to man's conviction—learned in a Bible-centered culture—that the universe was created by a

Can We Test The Bible's Claims?

rational and orderly God, and therefore its workings could be discovered and harnessed because they were reliable.

Perhaps most important, only those who know the Bible know that God is holy and just, and at the same time loving and merciful.

To quote Thiessen again: "When we consider the character of the Bible we are forced to come to but one conclusion. It is the embodiment of a divine revelation.[9]

Testable Evidence

The God who invites us to come and reason together with Him has not left us without ways to test His claims. We do not have to accept His Word on "blind faith." Whenever He spoke to man, He graciously gave evidence that He was who He said He was. Moses' miraculous rod and the ten plagues validated him as Jehovah's spokesman. The miracle of the wet and dry fleece assured Gideon. Elijah was vindicated by the victory on Mount Carmel. Other examples are too numerous to list.

Just so He has given us evidences that the Bible is exactly what it claims to be—His communication to man.

Fulfilled prophecy. The entire Bible is a prophetic Book, but it is not without reason that Isaiah has been called the prince of prophets. In chapters 41-46 we have Jehovah's extended challenge to His people to put away their idols and return to Him because of who He is. Who else, He asks, can tell you not only what happened in the remotest past, but also what will happen in the remotest future? If He pronounces it, it will come to pass: "My counsel shall stand, and I will do all my pleasure" (Isaiah 46:10).

It was because this omniscient God spoke through the Bible writers that we can test its claims to be His infallible revelation. The test of a true prophet has always been, Can he foretell the future? The Bible prophets first had to validate their claims to their own generation. They made short-term prophecies that their contemporaries saw fulfilled. But God gave them long-range prophecies also that would come to pass only in future generations, so that His dealings with man might be validated. We will look at just a few of the more prominent ones.

One hundred and fifty years before it happened, Isaiah foretold the work of Cyrus the Persian. This prophecy is recorded in Isaiah 44:24—45:4. Its fulfillment, which occurred nearly two hundred years later, is recorded in Ezra 1:1-4.

When Jeroboam, the first ruler of the northern kingdom of Israel, built a golden calf at Bethel, an unnamed prophet forecast that it would be destroyed by a king descended from David and named Josiah. Three hundred years later, King Josiah did destroy the altar at Bethel, and only after having done so did he learn about the prophecy. The prophet's words are recorded in 1 Kings 13:1-3, and the fulfillment is in 2 Kings 23:15-18.

Nahum prophesied that Nineveh would be destroyed and never rebuilt (Nahum 2:1-13). Isaiah predicted the downfall of Babylon so that it would be uninhabited and a place for "the Arabian to pitch his tent and wild beast dwell there" (Isaiah 13:20). These cities have vanished just as prophesied. Prophecies against Tyre, Edom and other ancient places could just as well be cited.

Most remarkable of all, however, are the hundreds of prophecies concerning the coming of Christ that have been fulfilled. Thirty-three came true on the day of the crucifixion alone. The gospel writers are careful to point out these instances with phrases such as, "That the Scripture might be fulfilled."

It was the evidence of fulfilled prophecy that led to the conversion of the great second century apologist, Justin Martyr.

Corroboration from Archaeology. The Bible is a book of theology; that is, its message concerns God's dealings with man. Much of it, therefore, is not subject to corroboration. However, when in the course of presenting this message it touches on matters of history, geography, custom and other earthly things, it can be checked out by extra-biblical evidence.

For example, a study of cognate languages (that is, languages

Can We Test The Bible's Claims?

related to Hebrew) throws a great deal of illumination on individual words and ancient customs. There have also been numerous instances of general corroboration; that is, without referring to specific people or events, the background fits so remarkably that we recognize the authors of the text knew what they were talking about. Archaeologists have discovered, for example, that if they uncover a city the Bible says existed in Abraham's day, the evidence shows that it really did. Cities not mentioned during his time show no evidence of habitation during that era. This is true even of cities which thrived before Abraham's day, fell into ruins, and after his time were again inhabited. This type of corroboration furnishes strong arguments for refuting the documentary hypothesis so generally accepted today even by some writers of Sunday school material.

More remarkable are the numerous occasions where challenges to the trustworthiness of the text or of the early date of a book of the Bible have been conspicuously corroborated by archaeology. A very few examples: forgotten kings have been discovered in extra-Biblical documents. Belshazzer is one. It was once claimed that history gave no evidence of such a Babylonian king. More recent discoveries have shown that he was co-ruler with his father who left him in charge of the province of Babylon. Obviously, the reason he offered to make Daniel "third ruler in the kingdom" (Daniel 5:16) was because he himself was only second.

Difficulties in lining up the chronology of the kings of Israel and Judah have been cleared away. The Book of Acts, which critics long sought to turn into a second century writing, has been shown to contain geographical references that were true of the first century but not of the second. The discovery of a fragment of the gospel of John demonstrated that it could not have been written, as the critics accused, long after the apostles' lifetimes.

The newly discovered ruins of Ebla show early promise of producing many more such exciting corroborations.

Because the Scripture has shown itself to be so trustworthy in its references to these "earthly things," they are the more without excuse who refuse to trust what it has to say about eternal matters.

Argument from changed lives. The resurrection of Jesus Christ is often called the miracle of miracles. If we can accept that, no other problem in the Bible is difficult. Although Jesus had foretold it (another evidence of fulfilled prophecy), not even His disciples were ready to expect or believe it. Yet, when they were convinced, it changed them from frightened fugitives into martyred apostles.

Consider also the changed life of the apostle Paul after his meeting with the risen Lord. He had everything—in a worldly sense—to gain by rejecting Christ and the fact of His resurrection, and everything to lose by accepting Him. Yet he gave up all his hopes of wealth and prestige to accept scourging, suffering, perils, trials, and ultimate martyrdom for the truth of the gospel. Lord Lyttleton said, "The conversion and apostleship of St. Paul alone, duly considered, was of itself a demonstration sufficient to prove Christianity to be a divine revelation."[10]

From the apostles' time to our own, the evidence of changed lives has been one of the most powerful arguments for recognizing the Bible as God's revelation to man. Paul himself had much to say in his epistles about the changed lives of believers, but it is pretty well summed up in 2 Corinthians 5:17, "Therefore if any man be in Christ, he is a new creature; old things are passed away; behold all things are become new."

An interesting example of the convincing power of changed lives was once told by the late Dr. Harry Ironside. He was working with the Salvation Army doing street preaching when a prosporous-looking atheist who had stopped to listen offered to debate him in the park the following Sunday afternoon. Ironside accepted on one condition—that the atheist bring with him one hundred people whose lives had been transformed by the power of atheism. He himself would bring one hundred on which

Can We Test The Bible's Claims?

the power of the gospel had wrought that miracle. He turned to the Salvation Army captain, asking, "Can you help me round them up by that time?"

"Certainly," replied the captain. "I can get at least forty from just our own chapter, and a brass band to lead them to the park." The atheist backed down.

All who have eyes to see and a mind to reason can know for themselves the evidences that the Bible is an infallible revelation from God. Its prophecies are still being fulfilled. Archaeologists are digging up the ancient past and finding it just as the biblical writers said it was. And all around us are lives that have been transformed by the power of the Word of God.

SUMMARY

In addition to the internal testimony of Scripture itself concerning its infallibility, we can test many of its earthly claims by our reason and observation. The character of God and the influence of the Scripture on human affairs are weighty arguments that God is its source.

Furthermore, the undeniable facts of fulfilled prophecy and the discoverable facts of history, geography and archaeology are testimony to the trustworthiness of Scripture.

These external evidences are no "proof" of the Bible, but, taken together, the weight of their combined reason provides valuable evidence to the open-minded that the claims of those who teach the human fallibility of the Bible have no basis in fact.

FOOTNOTES

[1] Heb. 1:1, 2
[2] Acts 17:28; 1 Cor. 15:33; Titus 1:12
[3] Gen. 1:27
[4] Gen. 2:20
[5] Henry C. Thiessen, *Introductory Lectures in Systematic Theology*. Grand Rapids, Mich.: Wm. B. Eerdmans Publishing Co., 1949, p. 81.
[6] Eccl. 12:12
[7] Jer. 36:20-26

[8] W. F. Albright, "The Old Testament and Archaeology." In *Old Testament Commentary*, H. C. Alleman and E. E. Flack, eds. Philadelphia: The Muhlenberg Press, 1948, p. 135.

[9] Thiessen, Op. cit., p. 85.

[10] "Observations on the Life of St. Paul," published in *The Works of George Lord Lyttleton*. London: George Edward Ayscough, 1774, p. 271.

Chapter 4

How Do Some Attempt To Undermine The Trustworthiness Of Scripture?

When one accepts the fact that the Bible is the personal and objective revelation of God's will to man, he is immediately faced with certain very basic consequences. The first is that, since this is the Word of God, it must therefore be infallible; that is, there can be absolutely no error in any part of it. Jesus confirmed this conclusion when He said in His high priestly prayer, "Thy Word is Truth."[1]

The second conclusion is that, being God's revelation, the Bible is therefore authoritative; that is, we are bound to believe and obey it. As James commands, we must be "doers of the Word, and not hearers only."[2]

But, man, being sinful, does not want to accept the Scripture as having such absolute authority over his life—his behavior as well as his belief—and so he seeks for ways to circumvent these conclusions. Someone has put it that men do not reject the Bible because it contradicts itself, but because it contradicts them. A recent report on the annual conference of a major denomination provides an example of this when a vote was taken to accept a controversial study on sexuality that "advocated a view that the Bible alone is not an adequate guide for morality or sexual conduct."[3] Among other things, the study objected to the Bible's condemnation of homosexual acts and of sex outside of marriage. It passed by a two-thirds majority.

In this chapter we will look at some of the ways men have attempted to undermine the trustworthiness of the Scripture, and consider the weaknesses of these efforts.

Anti-Evangelical Positions

Included in this category are all those who elevate reason above revelation, who seek natural explanations for all supernatural events of Scripture thereby downgrading the supernatural and the Bible miracles. Such individuals have difficulty with the great Bible doctrines such as the Virgin Birth and the Resurrection. As one professor at a liberal seminary put it, "It is not that I believe God couldn't do such a thing; it is just that I don't believe He works that way."

Liberal or "Modernist" Viewpoints. Old-style modernists will go no further than to say that the Bible *contains* the Word of God. They are not always in agreement among themselves as to what this means. Some suggest that from time to time God granted to deeply pious men a special insight into His truth, and that this insight or illumination appears in their writings. Theologians refer to it as "the illumination view." The professor referred to above, when asked what he meant when he said the Old Testament prophets were inspired, replied that they were inspired in much the same way as was Shakespeare.

Others, who are even less willing to give God any initiative action, suggest that the natural religious insight of some devout and deep-thinking men enabled them to grasp divine truth beyond the reach of most of us, and that they recorded these insights for posterity. This is referred to theologically as the intuition view. It is illustrated in textbooks for elementary social studies which suggest that early men, being largely keepers of flocks and herds, in their long nights of meditation as they watched over their animals, began to think there must be Someone who exercised the same care over men. Thus they began to develop a concept of God which they passed on to their posterity.

Christians cannot accept these liberal viewpoints. They are man-centered, suggesting that man *discovers* truth rather than that God *reveals* it. It allows human reason to sit in judgment on the Bible in determining what parts are divine truth and what are totally human thinking. Furthermore, they take naturalism[4] as a presupposition, excluding God. They may permit God to be the Creator of His universe, but not its sustainer. In these viewpoints, He left it to run by itself. Finally, and most important, the theory must be rejected because it is not biblical. We saw in chapter 2 how the entire Old and New Testament claims emphatically to be the revealed Word of God.

Neo-orthodox view. The old-fashioned nineteenth century liberals said that the Bible *contains* the Word of God. Twentieth century liberalism, popularly known as neo-orthodoxy, suggests that the Bible *becomes* the Word of God when one is personally confronted with it in a meaningful encounter.

Karl Barth is considered the founder of this school of thinking. He and others like him became disillusioned with the old liberal belief in the perfectability of man on his own. Some suggest that these ideals died when the horrors of World War I demonstrated how far man is from reaching them. Barth and others began preaching a divine revelation and an authoritative Bible. They had, however, been educated by the old liberals and failed to break away from Wellhausen and his Documentary Hypothesis[5] concerning the origin of the Bible. They were also schooled in Kierkegaard's Existentialism.[6]

With this background they developed the proposition that God chose to use the Bible, even though it was human and imperfect, to confront men through a personal encounter to which it would speak to him meaningfully and concretely. To such theologians the Bible is not objectively God's Word whether or not anyone is listening; it only *becomes* God's Word by means of an existential encounter. Emil Brunner is credited with coining the terms "bibliolatry" and "paper pope" in his rejection of belief in an objective and infallible revelation.

A more radical version of neo-orthodoxy, best exemplified by

Rudolph Bultmann, called for the "demythologizing" of Scripture. In other words, the Bible must be stripped of its cultural overtones (meaning mostly its supernatural elements) in order to get at the core of truth. These teachers distinguish between factual literal history and "religious" history. By this they mean that the history recorded in the Bible concerning the Fall, the Crucifixion and the Resurrection as well as the many miraculous events is "real" through not necessarily "factual" because if we look beyond the merely historical with its errors and myths to the "super-history," we can find the core of truth of God's absolute love revealed in Christ.

The neo-orthodox viewpoint results in the improbable conclusion that the Bible can be inspired by God and at the same time contain error. Like the older liberals it also allows man to sit in judgment on what God has spoken, for who is to make the final decision as to which events presented as history are factual and which are mythological? More important, it downgrades the authority of Christ who accepted it all as simple history. On numerous occasions He cited Old Testament events and people as factual, including Abel, Noah and the flood, Abraham, the brazen serpent, Jonah and the repentance of Nineveh. After making a long list that included these and other citations, John W. Wenham notes how they reveal that Jesus took them as real people and incidents, and not mythical. He concludes:

> Although these quotations are taken by our Lord more or less at random from different parts of the Old Testament and some periods of the history are covered more fully than others, it is evident that he was familiar with most of our Old Testament and that he treated it all equally as history. Curiously enough, the narratives that are least acceptable to the so-called 'modern mind' are the very ones that he seemed most fond of choosing for his illustrations.[7]

Further, Jesus said to Nicodemus, "If I have told you earthly things and ye believe not, how shall ye believe if I tell you heavenly things?"[8] If we cannot believe He speaks the truth when He talks of matters that are subject to human verification, what assurance have we that He speaks truth in what He says about matters relating to our eternal destiny? We would soon find singing "Blessed Assurance" to be a meaningless piece of emotionalism instead of a bedrock conviction.

Some Conservative Views

Even those who accept Scripture as a direct revelation from God are not fully agreed as to the method of that revelation. Some of their explanations are even sub-biblical. It must be emphasized, however, that contrary to the liberal or neo-orthodox viewpoints, these views are held by Christian brethren fully committed to an objective revelation and faith in a resurrected Lord and Saviour whose shed blood is our only way of salvation.

The dictation view. It is almost impossible to find an evangelical or fundamentalist who claims to hold this view, but it is the view which fundamentalists are most commonly accused by their opposition of espousing. It reduces the biblical authors to the status of mere stenographers taking down their writing word for word as God dictated it to them. Such a viewpoint deprives Moses, the prophets, Paul and the rest of any right to be called human authors of the books credited to them. This is not in accordance with Scripture which not only recognizes the human writers of the books as being authors (as in the opening greetings of Paul's letters), but which reveals their individual personalities, experiences, temperaments and literary styles in a way that is not so for a stenographer.

Since God's written Word, like His living Word, is both fully divine and fully human (yet without human error), this viewpoint fails to do justice to the humanity of the Scripture just as much as the liberal view fails to do justice to the divine.

The dynamic view. Whereas dictation downplays the human aspect of Scripture, this view runs the risk of over-humanizing it. According to this concept God did not inspire His prophets with words, but with thoughts and ideas which they put into their own words.

We cannot say, of course, in what ways communication may

be carried on within the Trinity, or between God and His angels. We do know, however, that man can receive and transmit communication only by means of concrete symbols, of which words are the most universal. This is why it is so meaningful that God should call both His written and His living revelation His Word. The God who created us knew how to reveal Himself to us by clothing His thoughts in symbols we can receive and understand. Words may take the form of either audible or visible symbols, or even, as in the famous case of Helen Keller, tactile ones, but some such concrete embodiment of one's thoughts must be made if communication is to take place.

The neo-evangelical view. This view represents the most current effort of evangelical believers to present a doctrine of Scripture that is not offensive to the intellectual mind and does not require disagreement with the world of science. Consciously or unconsciously, the desire to be intellectually respectable appears to be a moving force behind this viewpoint.

Those who espouse this view claim to accept the historic creeds of the church which state that the Bible is our infallible rule for faith and practice (or belief and behavior). However, they boggle at the term inerrancy and hedge it by stating that Scripture is inerrant (meaning without error) in all that it affirms relative to our faith and practice, but that when it speaks of history, science, etc. this is purely incidental and must be understood in the light of the times in which it was written.

This position makes the word *inerrancy* a meaningless term and makes its adherents less than candid in their efforts to be counted both among those who hold to an inerrant revelation and those who accept the philosophies of the modern scientists, psychologists and others. The dangers of this viewpoint have been most fully exposed by Harold Lindsell.[9] The virulance of the attacks against Lindsell and the accusations that he is dividing Christians shows clearly how strongly evangelical intellectuals have become wedded to this concept.

Who is to decide what is "religious" and what is "incidental" in the biblical revelation? Again, man is allowing himself to sit refers to such "incidental" matters as history, geography or science.

A true biblical view of Scripture must recognize that we have a revelation from God, transmitted through chosen men, in which the very words were inspired but not dictated, and which is both fully divine and fully human.

FOOTNOTES

[1] John 17:17
[2] James 1:22
[3] See *Christianity Today*, Aug. 12, 1977, p. 38.
[4] Theologically, this is the teaching that all religious truths may be learned from observation of the world of nature, and that true religion does not depend on supernatural experience.
[5] This is the theory accepted by most liberal theologians that the Pentateuch was really a compilation of a number of independent documents produced centuries apart and brought together long after the lifetime of Moses. They usually designated the authors as J (because he preferred to call God Jehovah), E (because he preferred to call God Elohim), P (because it was supposedly written by a priest or priests and is supportive of the priesthood and sacrificial system), and D (because he was responsible for most of Deuteronomy which he wrote about the time of Josiah and palmed off as the lost book of God). It is often called the JEPD theory, and a basic grasp of it will help you understand the confusing references often made to the Bible in popular newspaper and magazine articles.
[6] Existentialism is the philosophy that stresses man's self-awareness and freedom. It focuses on his awareness of himself in his personal moment of history. A popular application of this philosophy is the so-called "situation ethics" which teaches that right and wrong are not absolutes, but depend on the total situation (including the motivation) in which an individual performs an act.
[7] *Christ and the Bible*. Downers Grove, Ill.: Inter-Varsity Press, 1972, p. 17.
[8] John 3:11
[9] *The Battle for the Bible*. Grand Rapids: Zondervan Publishing House, 1976.
[10] John 10:35
[11] Col. 2:3

Chapter 5

How Do We Know What Books Are Scripture?

Development of the Canon—Old Testament

The first link in the chain of the revelation of God's Word to man is inspiration—i.e., Scripture is God-breathed (2 Timothy 3:16). The second link is canonization. Inspiration provides the Scriptures with authority; canonization provides them with recognition or acceptance. In short, the story of canonization is the story of how certain writings were accepted as God's Word, while at the same time others were rejected.

"Canon" comes from the Greek word *kanon*, which originally meant rod, rule, staff, or measuring rod. It became used metaphorically to mean standard or norm. Thus, even in pre-Christian times its meaning was expanding. However, Christians used the word as a theological term meaning "rule of faith," or "normative writing." When applied to the Scripture, it came to mean those books accepted as being God-breathed.

To say that certain books were canonized means that they were accepted as being up to the standard or rule. Another illustration of the use of the word is in the canonizing of a saint by the Roman Catholic Church: they have officially decided that the individual has lived up to the standards they set for sainthood. (Of course, we reject this concept because we say the standard is too limited—all Christians are "called saints.").

The Recognition of the Old Testament Canon

From ancient times the Jews have revered Ezra the scribe as the one most responsible for assembling the sacred Old Testament books into their final form, and probably himself writing both Chronicles and Ezra-Nehemiah, incorporating Nehemiah's memoirs into the latter. He is described as one whose life was dedicated to the service of God's Word—"knowing," "doing," and "teaching" it (Ezra 7:10). Since the generally accepted date for his journey to Jerusalem is 444 B.C., his ministry provides support for the position of conservative theologians that the Old Testament canon was complete four centuries before the birth of Christ. You will recall from chapter 2 that, according to the Hebrew order of books, the Old Testament closes with Ezra, Nehemiah and Chronicles.

Although they had no word equivalent to "canon," the Jews even before Christ recognized certain books as possessing a special status different from all others. Moses had commanded that the Torah be kept in the ark of the covenant. However, when Solomon installed the ark in his newly-built temple, he found it contained only the stone tablets of the Law.[1] So, the original was lost by his time. We are not told whether he added a copy of the Torah. In any event, the ark itself was lost in the destruction of Jerusalem by Nebuchadnezzar in 586 B.C.

The idea of the ark as the proper container for the Torah was preserved by the synagogues that sprang up during the exile, so that in time the cabinet which held the rolls of Scripture was called the ark. Thus we know that the Jews from earliest times regarded certain writings as sacred.

David instructed Solomon to keep the Law.[2] Ezra also revered, studied and taught certain writings as "the law of the Lord."[3] We know both from the Talmud and from evidence at Qumran[4] that some writings were regarded as so sacred they defiled the hand that handled them. Perhaps the most important source for the recognition of the uniqueness of Scripture at an early time is the first century A.D. Jewish historian, Josephus, who said

How Do We Know What Books Are Scripture?

> From Artaxerxes until our time everything has been recorded, but has not been deemed worthy of like credit with what preceded, because the exact succession of the prophets ceased. But what faith we have placed in our own writings is evident by our conduct for though so long a time has now passed, no one has dared to add anything to them or take anything away from them, or to alter anything in them.[5]

Since Artaxerxes was the Persian ruler who sponsored the return of Ezra and Nehemiah to Jerusalem, this statement supports the conservative position that the Canon was closed in the time of Ezra.

Josephus is also significant because he is an independent non-Christian ancient source who antedates the Talmud. Note the last words—that no one dared to add or to take anything away. This certainly shows that the writings had the status of canonicity for first century Jews.

Explanations for the Formation of the Old Testament Canon

1. Some have suggested that the Old Testament canon simply came into being as Jews came to revere their ancient heritage and the writers of the past—that age was the main reason the Canon was collected. This is an inadequate explanation because we know by name many ancient books that were not preserved, some even having been written by prophets. Examples are The Book of the Wars of Jehovah, The Book of Jasher, The Book of Nathan the Prophet, The Prophecy of Abijah the Shilomite, The Visions of Iddo the Seer.[6] Some of these may actually have been quoted in the canonical books, but it is clear that whatever was quoted was quoted correctly and became part of the Canon.

It is also noteworthy that many younger books; for example, Ezra-Nehemiah and the post-exilic prophets, are included in the Canon. So age could not have been the determining factor.

2. Related to the above theory is the suggestion that survival may have been the reason for books entering the Canon. This cannot be true because we know that many surviving books

existed among the Dead Sea Scrolls that did not enter the Canon.

3. Still others have said that the key to preservation in the Canon is the fact that a given book was written in Hebrew. There are two very important reasons for rejecting this conclusion. First, there are writings not in Hebrew included in the Old Testament (parts of Ezra and Daniel). Second, many books written in Hebrew have survived but are not in the Canon; for example, Ecclesiasticus, Maccabees, and other books of the Apocrypha, as well as a number found among the Dead Sea Scrolls.

4. Another theory suggests that books were accepted into the Canon if they agreed with the Torah of Moses. True, all the canonical writings do agree with him. But again, we know of others that also agree but are not included. Furthermore, it is unlikely that one of the prophets who we know to be a man of God, such as Elijah, and who we know wrote a book,[7] would not have written in agreement with the Torah. So this fact alone cannot have been the determining one.

5. Others suggest that the Old Testament canon was determined by the religious value of a given book. Here we have a very subjective concept that is difficult to evaluate. After all, only books with religious value would enter the Canon in any event. Then, there are books of the Apocrypha whose religious value is rich (e.g. Ecclesiasticus), yet no Protestant today would include them. Like the question of being in agreement with the Torah, this consideration alone would be an insufficient basis for determining canonicity.

6. A final and popular suggestion is that the Canon was determined by some church council or Jewish synod. In the first place, this makes a tremendous assumption that since church councils played a part in ratifying church doctrine and recognizing canonical New Testament books, that therefore the Jews did so. Evidence of any such activity is lacking.

It is true that before the fall of Jerusalem in A.D. 70, a famous member of the Sanhedrin left the besieged city and begged

How Do We Know What Books Are Scripture?

Titus, the Roman general, to let a scholar pass in peace and be permitted to make Jamnia—a town near Joppa—neutral turf where Jewish scholars might continue to teach in peace. Titus granted the request, and after the fall of Jerusalem the Sanhedrin was re-established at Jamnia to carry on its ecclesiastical functions. Many years later the Talmud records that it was here discussion arose as to whether certain books (sometimes called the *antilegomena*[8]) were really to be accepted. Song of Solomon was challenged because it struck some as too sensual. Ecclesiastes seemed too skeptical. Esther did not contain the name of God. Ezekial was charged with being anti-Moses because some teachings in the first ten chapters were thought to reveal Gnostic tendencies. Finally, Proverbs was charged with self-contradictions.[9] In the end, all the books prevailed because they were regarded as defiling the hands and had acceptance from the past. This discussion was not an act of canonization, but only of recognizing an established fact.

R. Laird Harris cites a study by Jack P. Lewis that demonstrates how the liberal critics have made too much of the so-called council of Jamnia.[10]

In contrast to these less than adequate explanations, the following facts are significant:

As we have already seen, the words of Moses were recognized in his lifetime as being the words of God. Thus we may say that the canonicity of his writings was determined by God, men only recognizing this already intrinsic authority. They were not elevated to their unique position by men, but belonged there because God spoke them. Israel had witnessed the plagues, the parting of the Red Sea, and knew that God talked with Moses at Sinai. It was not difficult for them to recognize Moses' writings as the Word of God. From the time of Joshua these five books were accepted as God's word—His *Torah* or Law. This is made explicit in Joshua 1:8 and is reiterated throughout the book by comments like, "as I said unto Moses," and similar phrases.

Harris has also made some interesting suggestions concerning the continuity of prophetic revelation.[11] He notes that there is a built-in continuity among the historical books of the Old Testament. For example, Ezra repeats the last two verses of Kings. Kings begins with the death of David, which had ended Samuel. Ruth (which may have originally been appended to Judges) ends with a genealogy that connects to David. Judges 1 repeats some events of Joshua. And, finally, the two most disputed connecting passages of all—the death of Joshua in chapter 24 of his book, and the death of Moses in Deuteronomy 12.

These two have been the cause of much contention because of the problem that if Moses wrote the Torah and Joshua his book, how could they have described their own deaths? Some have needlessly asserted the gift of prophecy, but Harris suggests it is explained by the continuance of a prophetic office. Since ancient books were written on scrolls or tablets, lengthy works required many scrolls or tablets. In order to keep them in order, the technique was to write the last line over at the beginning of the next in the series. Thus Joshua may well have given the Torah its completed form with the death of Moses so he could begin his account with, "Now after the death of Moses . . ."

In like manner, the elders Joshua left to judge Israel may have added the last five verses to his complete work to give it a similar conclusion. It was then put beside the Torah in the ark. Then, beginning with Samuel as the line of prophets took up the continuing account of the history of God's dealings with his people, the other books were added to the collection. Samuel may well have written Judges-Ruth as an introduction to Samuel. Since Chronicles credits other prophets with writing history, Samuel and Kings probably contain their work. Some passages in Kings are almost verbatim in Isaiah and Jeremiah.[12] The books bearing their names may be the collected works of these prophets in which were automatically included their own additions to the prophetic account of Israel's history. The writings of these prophets were accepted on a par with Moses because they had been validated according to his standard.[13]

Is it possible that some prophecies and inspired words of the prophets are lost? Of course; it is probable. Just as many sermons of our Lord during His ministry were never recorded. John 21:25 is very specific about this: "And there are also many other things which Jesus did, the which, if they should be written every one, I suppose that even the world itself could not contain the books that should be written." They were no less God's Word for being forgotten, but God in His providence has preserved those accounts and words He chose to for our example and profit.[14]

The Arrangement of the Old Testament Canon

The books of the Bible follow two basic arrangements. Our English Bible uses that of the Greek Septuagint, often called the Alexandrian Canon. The Hebrew arrangement is called the Palestinean Canon.[15]

A popular (but unacceptable) liberal theory. In popular publications, such as certain syndicated Sunday school lessons, we often find writers who maintain that the three divisions of the Hebrew Bible represent three stages of canonization: The Torah, canonized 400 B.C., the Prophets, canonized 200 B.C., and the Writings, canonized A.D. 90 (time of the council of Jamnia). This theory requires late dating of the books in each division. This late dating is itself based on further assumptions—that it is not possible anyone could have had the gift of foretelling the future, rejecting of the miraculous, and acceptance of the Graf-Wellhausen evolutionary theory of the development of Scripture.[16] Harris, in the article previously cited, goes to considerable length to refute this theory, showing how frequently late books cite earlier books or verses in them, which the liberal theorists insist are later than those cited.

The Green Theory. In opposition to the critical theory above, William Henry Green of Princeton (about 1890) came out with a substitute explanation of the three divisions. The Torah, of course, stands apart and at the head because it is Mosaic and the oldest part of Scripture. Green proposed that the later books were put together in two collections—the prophets and the writings. Those classified as prophets were those who had not only the gift of prophecy but also the office of prophet, while the other writers, although they possessed the gift of prophecy, had other secular offices—kings, civil servants, etc. This view has been widely accepted among evangelicals and is the popular conservative explanation.

The MacRae-Harris Theory. Laird Harris cites Dr. Allan MacRae (now of Biblical Seminary) as not being happy with the Green theory and suggesting that the divisions might rather have had their origin in the liturgical use of Scripture in the synagogue.[17] Harris notes that some books, like Daniel, were called prophecies by both Christ and Josephus. Lamentations was by Jeremiah, so according to Green it should be in the second division. Ruth was often attached to Judges and hence in the second division. Josephus lists only poetical books in his third division. The five books of the Megilloth[18] are clearly grouped together for liturgical reasons—namely, to be read in order on five successive feast days. So it is possible that the liturgical use of Scripture may have influenced the arrangement.

Noting that in the first century A.D. books were still on scrolls, Harris suggests that their arrangement and groupings may have been fluid, and that it was not until the invention of the bound book that their order became fixed.

The rejected books. There remain two collections of books that are not accepted by Protestants as being Scripture. These are the Apocrypha and the Pseudopigrapha (false writings). The eighteen books of the Pseudopigrapha are books whose authorship is uncertain. Most of them claim to be by some famous person of the past; e.g., Enoch, Solomon, one of the twelve sons of Jacob. The claims are obviously false. All were written late and have not been accepted as canonical by anyone.

The word Apocrypha means "secret" or "hidden," but the meaning seems to have little to do with the collection so titled.

How Do We Know What Books Are Scripture?

Some are historical, some didactic, some romantic, some prophetic and some legendary. In 1564 the Roman Catholic Church at the Council of Trent officially accepted them as Scripture. No church father before Augustine of Hippo accepted them, and some interpret him as only recommending them as valuable reading. The Roman church finds them of value in supporting teachings rejected by the Reformers. Protestantism has almost forgotten them since the Bible Society of London about 1821 dropped them from their position between the Testaments.

It has been argued in their favor that the apocryphal books were part of the Alexandrian Canon, but this was based on the text of the fourth century A.D. codexes. Where they stood in the minds of Alexandrian Jews five centuries earlier cannot be argued from that. A dozen arguments may be marshalled against them, but suffice it to say they were not acccepted by the early church nor by the Jews. They contain inaccuracies and inconsistencies. Many are fanciful. When read they do not have the ring of Scripture. However, they include much important history and are worth reading at least once.

In conclusion, it must be emphasized again that the hand of God is evident in the collection of the Canon. He has given us the record of all His words and acts in history that are necessary for our knowledge of Him, of salvation, and growth to Christian maturity. The completed Old Testament is one message with one unifying theme—Christ is coming!

SUMMARY

The Old Testament as we have it was recognized as canonical (our God-given "rule" of faith and practice) from the time each book was written. It was probably complete by 400 B.C. in essentially the same form as we now have it. Any explanation that makes men or groups of men the arbiters of what constitutes the Canon is inadequate and should be rejected.

The manner in which the books of the second and third divisions are arranged, and even into which division they fall, is a different matter. They have come down to us in more than one sequence, a fact probably best explained by the way they were used in the synagogue services.

The most important thing is to know that the Holy Spirit has inerrantly preserved all that is necessary for our profit and example.

FOOTNOTES

[1] 1 Kings 8:9
[2] 1 Kings 2:3
[3] Ezra 7:10
[4] The site of the discovery of the Dead Sea Scrolls
[5] *Contra Apion* 1:9
[6] Num. 21:14; Josh. 10:13; 2 Sam. 1:18; 2 Chron. 9:29
[7] 2 Chron. 21:12
[8] Canonical books about which there was some early dispute (however, chiefly used in reference to the New Testament canon).
[9] Prov. 26:4,5
[10] *Zondervan's Pictorial Encyclopedia of the Bible*, I, 725
[11] *Ibid.*, pp. 715-718
[12] Cf. 2 Kings 18:17—20:20 and Isa. 36—39; also 2 Kings 24:18—25:30 and Jer. 39:1-10; 40:7-10; 44:1-3; 52:1-34
[13] Deut. 18:15-22
[14] 1 Cor. 10:4,11; 2 Tim. 3:16
[15] See chaper 2
[16] This theory was briefly sketched in chapter 3
[17] Harris credits unpublished notes from Dr. MacRae's classes for this information
[18] See chart, chapter 2

Chapter 6

How Do We Know What Books Are Scripture?

Development of the Canon—New Testament
I have yet many things to say unto you, but ye cannot bear them now. Howbeit when he, the Spirit of truth, is come, he will guide you into all truth; for he shall not speak of himself, but whatsoever he shall hear, that shall he speak; and he will show you things to come. (John 16:12-13).

So spoke Jesus to His disciples on the night of his betrayal, but they did not yet understand what he meant. At that moment in time those men regarded themselves as good Jews. They accepted the twenty-four books of the Old Testament Scriptures. They attended the synagogue and temple services. They revered their Master as the Messiah promised by the Old Testament prophets. But they did not yet dream that they themselves would exercise the ancient prophetic gift and add to the canon of Scripture. It took the shock of the events of the next few hours, followed by the triumph of the resurrection and forty days of post-resurrection teaching to change them from disciples (learners) to apostles (sent ones) who through the foolishness of their preaching would turn the world upside down.

The New Testament was Written with Expectation of Being Received and Obeyed
We have seen that the development of the Old Testament canon was shrouded in antiquity. We are dependent primarily

upon its claims for itself and what the New Testament says about it. The New Testament, on the contrary, springs as it were from the garden tomb into the full light of the Golden Age of Rome. The New Testament books were written in a highly literate age to intelligent people who lived in a culture that challenged the veracity of all things. In that respect their era was much like our own.

The Holy Spirit guided the formation of the canon so that four questions could be answered: 1. What were the facts of the life of Christ? 2. How did the early church grow and spread? 3. How should these facts be interpreted and applied to daily life? 4. What will be the consummation of all things? The New Testament, in other words, is the charter of the Christian church. Its foundation is laid in the Gospels. Its formation is described in Acts. Its function is explained in the Epistles. Its future is revealed in the Book of Revelation. (see fig. 2.) It is vital, therefore, that we know how and why these books are distinct from the many other Christian writings of the early church, and why they were recognized and accepted as Scripture—the infallible Word of God.

The Gospels and Acts. In His promise of inspiration quoted above, Jesus said He would recall to the minds of His disciples all they needed to know in order to defend their message of truth.

In the beginning the gospel message spread by what Paul called "the foolishness of preaching."[1] The Christians—Jew and Gentile—possessed only the Old Testament Scriptures. This is what the people of Berea studied.[2] It was these that Peter, Stephen, Philip and others used as their texts from which to preach Christ.[3] The stories of Jesus' life, death and resurrection, as brought to mind by the Holy Spirit, were told and retold from memory until a kind of oral gospel circulated among the churches. This background may account for the similarities and differences in the telling of stories in the three synoptic[4] gospels, Matthew, Mark and Luke, being mindful, of course, of the Holy Spirit's role in guiding the various emphases.

How Do We Know What Books Are Scripture?

As time passed, and one by one the apostles were scattered and martyred, it became imperative that authoritative accounts from their hands be given to the church. It was probably from this base of oral teaching, coupled with their own personal knowledge and possibly some short written accounts that, guided by the Holy Spirit, the gospel writers produced their manuscripts. Some also believe Matthew may have taken notes during Jesus' ministry and these, being available to the others, help account for similarities in the synoptic gospels.

Whether Matthew or Mark was written first is disputed by fundamental scholars. There is interesting evidence from the caves of the Dead Sea Scrolls that the writing of the Gospels may have been undertaken within twenty years of the resurrection of Christ and before Paul's second missionary journey.[5] It is usually conceded that both Matthew and Mark preceded Luke. If the theory is correct that Luke wrote under Paul's guidance and was preparing an account of the origin and spread of the church (Luke-Acts) for use in Paul's defense at Rome, we may assume that all three synoptic accounts were complete by A.D. 61 or 62.

John may have written his gospel nearly a quarter century later, although some are now beginning to argue for an earlier date. His intention clearly was to answer heresies already growing up in the church, while at the same time presenting additional information not recorded in the synoptics, which were probably already circulating and known to him. The second century apologist, Iranaeus, in defending the truth against the Gnostic heresy, had this to say about the formation of the four Gospels:

> Matthew among the Hebrews issued a Writing of the gospel in their own tongue, . . . Mark, the disciple and interpreter of Peter, also handed down to us in writing what Peter had preached. Then Luke, the follower of Paul, recorded in a book the gospel as it was preached by him. Finally John, the disciple of the Lord . . himself published the Gospel, while he was residing at Ephesus in Asia.[6]

The Epistles and Revelation. Not only do we find that Christ promised the apostles inspiration, we find also throughout their writings that they themselves were conscious of being the instruments of inspiration.[7]

James is usually thought to be the earliest epistle written, probably prior to the Council of Jerusalem which took place about A.D. 49.[8] It is a general instruction from the leader of the Jerusalem church to the Christians who were already scattered abroad.[9]

Next (in the 50s) came Paul's letters of instruction to the struggling new churches he had founded. That Paul was conscious of his apostolic authority and spoke with the expectation that his words were to be received and obeyed as coming from Christ is particularly evident in his letters to the Corinthians; e.g. 1 Corinthians 4:14-21; 11:2; 14:37; 2 Corinthians 12:1-12. Significantly, it was the Corinthian church that most seriously questioned his authority.

In 1 Thessalonians 2:13, he commended the church for receiving his words as the Word of God. Note also how he described himself in Galations 1:1-8, as appointed by Christ, and then proceeded to lay down the basic principles of Christianity which, he said, might not be contradicted even by an angel from heaven.

We have already seen how 2 Peter dealt with inspiration (chapter 1) and put the apostolic stamp of Scripture authority on Paul's writings.[10]

At its beginning and end, Revelation promises a blessing on all who read it (Revelation 1:3; 22:7) and a curse on all who would add to or take away from its words (Revelation 22:18).

In writing his first letter to Timothy, Paul used the expression "Scripture saith" (1 Timothy 5:18) and then made two quotations, one from Deuteronomy 25:4 and the other from Luke 10:7, thus showing Old and New Testament passages as being equally Scripture. As we saw in chapter 1, Peter even placed the apostles on a par with the prophets[11] whose commandments were to be heeded. Peter then warned against

How Do We Know What Books Are Scripture?

scoffers coming in the last days. It is significant that Jude 17-18 cites this text to back up his argument.

John's epistles, like his gospel, must have been written years after Peter and Paul were martyred (about A.D. 68). Revelation is generally regarded as the last New Testament book written, probably during the persecution under the emperor Domnitian about A.D. 96.

To sum up this section we quote from Laird Harris:

> We come to the conclusion that Paul and the apostles were conscious that they wrote as men inspired by God. This was not merely their own conviction, but was in full accord with the promises which Christ had given them that they would be ordained by the Holy Spirit for just such a work. The gift of the Holy Spirit in the matter of revelation was fully supported by other gifts of the Spirit for the extensive healing ministries of the apostles recorded in the New Testament. Acts 2:43 speaks of the wonders and signs which were done by the apostles. Acts 5:13 says that after the death of Ananias and Sapphira the people magnified them, apparently in the context, the apostles. It is true that the New Testament speaks of an occasional miracle done in the New Testament by those not of the Twelve, but very few. Also there is an occasional prophecy of future events given by those not apostles but, again, these are exceptions. The apostles were evidently the spirit-ordained and recognized spokemen of God. Is it any wonder that the aspostle Paul can claim to speak in words taught of the Holy Spirit and can require that his writings should be received as the commandments of the Lord?[12]

The Recognition of the New Testament Canon

We have seen that the writers of Scripture recognized themselves as being in the prophetic succession. It remains to discover how and why the church recognized this claim and accepted their writings as Scripture (or as canonical).

Some stimuli for canonization. Even before the apostles passed from the scene, collections of their writings must have been under way. That Peter refers to such a collection of Paul's epistles seems apparent from 2 Peter 3:16. It need not have included all his epistles; 2 Timothy was probably not yet written at that time.

If hearing the gospel direct from the mouth of an apostle was valued, certainly any written word of theirs would be likewise valued. There existed in the church what has been called stimuli for canonization. First, the apostles were placed on a par with the prophets. Not only was this their own claim, as we have seen, it was also recognized by the men of the first post-apostolic generation whose writings have survived. For example, Clement of Rome, writing to the church at Corinth about A.D. 95 (possibly before Revelation was written), shows familiarity by quoting from or alluding to five of Paul's epistles (Romans, 1 Corinthians, Ephesians, 1 Timothy, Titus) as well as to James, John and Hebrews. His reference to 1 Corinthians is especially interesting.

> Take up the Epistle of the blessed Paul the apostle . . . in truth he spiritually charged you . . . [13]

This clearly shows that Paul's epistle to the Corinthians was already well known in Rome.

Second, the needs of the churches required a canon. The men who knew the apostles never placed themselves on a par with them, but sought to guide their churches theologically and spiritually by repeated readings and expositions of the words of the apostles. The church was born in apostolic preaching and grew by preaching based on the words of the apostles.

Third, there was a stimulus of growing heresy. The apostles themselves had to warn repeatedly against false teachers creeping in.[14] An authentic collection of apostolic writings was essential for the maintenance of sound doctrine.

Fourth, the missionary activity of the church meant that an accepted canon had to be translated into many other languages. While the earliest missionaries used Greek, it soon became necessary to translate the gospels into Latin and Syriac. As the centuries and churches multiplied, so did the languages.

Finally, persecution played its part as a stimulus to form a canon. The early removal of some of the apostles by martyrdom, and the expectation that such would be the end of them all, contributed an urgency that the Gospels and Epistles be recorded and collected for the guidance of the church. Peter's awareness of this need is evident from 2 Peter 1:13-15.

Guiding principles in the collection of the canon. Four principles seem to have functioned in the early church to guide their recognition of which books were canonical. (Note well: The church did not choose certain writing and make them canonical. They only recognized which books were intrinsically canonical because the Holy Spirit had inspired them.)

The first of the four principles was *apostolicity*. That is, was a given book written either by an apostle or under apostolic guidance? Thus, Matthew and John were accepted because they were written by apostles. Mark was accepted as being Peter's gospel recorded by him. (It is fascinating to read through this gospel giving special attention to the personal touches that must have come from Peter. This is especially obvious when his description of events is compared with the same event in the other synoptics.) Luke, though not an apostle, was accepted on the authority of Paul's apostleship. Likewise, Hebrews, though its authorship is not stated, was accepted as having been written either by Paul or under his authority. Ultimately it was added to the end of the collection of his epistles.

Secondly, there was the principle of *content*. Were they in agreement with apostolic teaching? On this basis an early work known as the Epistle of Barnabas was rejected even though it was highly valued by some early churches. It makes statements that imply salvation by works.

Third was the test of *universality*. Even such short and seemingly personal epistles as 2 and 3 John, when read with this test in mind, reveal a universal quality. It is quite possible that the apostles wrote personal letters that have not been preserved. It is even possible that they themselves recognized and discouraged the preservation of some epistles. This could explain what appears to be the two missing letters written by Paul to the Corinthians.[15]

Lastly, did the book give evidence of *inspiration*? Obviously, this is the most subjective and difficult test. No doubt, the Holy Spirit not only supervised the writing, but also the selection of the canon. Clearly the key test was apostolicity, since the apostles alone were given the unique status of equality with the prophets. This prophetic status was the key to apostolicity.

Recognition of the Canon. The first official recognition of the twenty-seven books of the New Testament canon by the church in council was given under St. Augustine's influence at Hippo (A.D. 393) and Carthage (A.D. 397). This has misled some into believing that the New Testament canon was a gradual development over four centuries. They fail to remember that in the first three centuries the bishops and other leaders of the church would not dare to assemble to discuss differences of opinion on doctrine or other issues because of recurring persecution. Under such circumstances, it is perhaps surprising how much general agreement there actually was. This was achieved primarily by the circulation of letters and other works. These are the prime sources of our realization that, although five New Testament books (James, 2 Peter, 2 and 3 John and Jude) were "spoken against" at the Council of Nicaea (A.D. 324), the first of the ecumenical councils, they were all recognized as canonical and cited authoritatively by the early church fathers of a much earlier date.

Today the adherents of some cults make it sound as though the councils were the "bad boys" who rooted out the true teachings of Christ (which they alone preserve). Actually the councils were called in order to state collectively what the church had been teaching. They are called "ecumenical" councils because church leaders from all over the world attended. The word did not have our present-day derogatory connotation.

Most interesting for the study of canonicity is the first century after the apostles. These men either knew and heard the apostles personally, or studied under men who did. Generally they are divided into two groups. Those active between A.D. 70 and 120 are called the apostolic fathers because of their

How Do We Know What Books Are Scripture?

probable contact with the apostles. Those writing between 120 and 170 are usually called the apologists because their writings were primarily in defense of the church and its doctrines.

From the first period we have epistles by Clement, bishop of Rome about A.D. 95, by Ignatius, bishop of Antioch, written as he traveled to his execution in Rome about A.D. 110, and by Ploycarp, bishop of Smyrna about 110-140, who claimed to have studied under the apostle John during that apostle's old age at Ephesus. From the same period is the epistle of Barnabas. Another witness on the latter edge of this period is Basilides, the Alexandrian Gnostic who, according to Eusebius, produced his works not long after the apostles and the Ophite Gnostics. R. Laird Harris quotes Westcott as saying:

> If it seems strange that the first direct proofs of a belief in the inspiration of the New Testament are derived from such a source, it may be remembered that it is more likely that the apologist of a suspicious system should support his argument by quotations from an authority acknowledged by his opponents than that a Christian teacher writing to fellow believers should insist on those testimonies with which he might suppose his reader to be familiar.[16]

These early writers cite authoritatively all the New Testament from Matthew to 1 John and Revelation. Ignored are only the three shortest epistles (perhaps because of their brevity). Figure 3 shows early references to the New Testament books in chart form.

In the period of the Greek apologists we have such men as Papias, Justin Martyr, Irenaeus (from who we quoted above), and again some heretics—Marcion and Valentinus. The popular Shepherd of Hermas probably also dates from this time, and it is also the era that saw the New Testament translated into the Old Latin and Old Syriac versions. Only Philemon, 2 John and 2 Peter are not cited in the writings of this period. Again, two of these are very short books and there may have been no occasion to refer to them. Second Peter, as we have seen, was already recognized in the earlier period. It is true that some questions as to its apostolicity were raised in the third and fourth centuries, but this was in spite of the fact that it had been widely recognized all the time.

We could now list the fathers of the third and fourth centuries, but while occasionally some books—Hebrews, James, 2 Peter, 2 and 3 John, Jude and Revelation—were questioned, all were indeed recognized, and had been recognized, by most of the church. Yet, since these were "spoken against" by some, critics have charged that the canon was not yet settled at that time. Such a charge is contrary to all the evidence that these books were indeed being cited as Scripture from the days of the apostolic fathers. To quote Harris again:

> Having traced the reception of the New Testament books back to the very edge of the apostolic times, we have found that there is evidence that practically all of them were accepted by the men who had learned from the apostles themselves.[17]

Eusebius tells us that Hegesippus (about 117-180), a Jewish Christian, traveled extensively and knew the church both in Corinth and in Rome, and that he found the same doctrine everywhere. Thiessen comments:

> The absence of any note of surprise or dissent in the writings of Hegesippus may be taken as a sign that he was accustomed to the recognition of the same books. It is clear that the canon goes back to the first century, even though it was almost the fifth before a church council recognized it.[18]

From the beginnings of Christianity the same teachings of the prophets and apostles that we can hold in our hands today have been the foundation and guiding charter of the church. Where it has been studied and obeyed the church has flourished; where it has been neglected she has become impotent. What we do with the Word of God will contribute to the church's effectiveness in our generation.

SUMMARY

The New Testament was recognized as cannonical from its inception.

From the New Testament itself we know that our Lord promised infallible recall to His apostles, that Paul wrote with the

How Do We Know What Books Are Scripture?

expectation of being accepted as the Word of God and that his churches did so accept his preaching, and that Peter placed the apostles, including Paul, on a par with the Old Testament prophets.

We have seen that the earliest Christian writers after the apostles accepted as normative for the church the same New Testament canon we have today, and that when the fourth and fifth century church councils labeled certain books as Scripture, they were only officially recognizing what had all along been the belief of the church.

There is no doubt but that the New Testament we have today is the same one that has guided the belief and behavior of the church from its beginnings.

FOOTNOTES

[1] 1Cor. 1:21
[2] Acts 17:11
[3] Acts 8:26-35 is one example.
[4] This term is applied to Matthew, Mark and Luke because they "see together" or develop their narratives from the same viewpoint and basic outline. They also major on the events of our Lord's ministry in Galilee wereas John gives much more space to the ministry in Judea, and especially Jerusalem.
[5] David Estrade & William White, Jr. *The First New Testament*. Nashville, N.Y.: Thomas Nelson, Inc., 1978.
[6] *Against Heresies*, Book III. Quoted from Cyril C. Richardson, ed., *Early Church Fathers*. New York: Macmillan Publishing Co.
[7] 1 Cor. 14:37; Gal. 1:18; 1 Thess. 2:13; 2 Peter 3:6
[8] Acts 15
[9] Acts 8:1; 11:19
[10] 2 Peter 3:15-16
[11] 2 Peter 3:2
[12] *Inspiration and Canonicity of the Bible*, pp. 232-33.
[13] Epistle to Corinth, quoted from Richardson, *op. cit.* p. 65.
[14] 1 Tim. 4:1-3; 2 Peter 2:1-3; 1 John 2:18-23; 4:1-3
[15] See 1 Cor. 5:9; 2 Cor. 2:3-9
[16] Harris, *op. cit.* p. 207.
[17] Wycliffe Bible Encyclopedia, I, p. 308.
[18] *Introduction to the New Testament*. Grand Rapids, Mich.: Wm. B. Eerdmans Publishing Co. 1943, p. 17.

NEW TESTAMENT
CHARTER OF THE CHURCH

Her FOUNDATION, the Gospels — What were the facts?
Her FORMATION, Acts — How did it spread?
Her FUNCTION, the Epistles — How should it be interpreted and applied?

Her FUTURE, Revelation — What will be the consummation?

Fig. 2

How Do We Know What Books Are Scripture?

RECOGNITION OF N.T. BOOKS DURING THE FIRST FOUR CENTURIES

x = Citation or allusion
O = Named as authentic
? = Named as disputed

	Apostolic Fathers	Greek Apologists	The 3rd and 4th Cent.
	Clement of Rome c.95 / Ignatius c.110 / Polycarp c.110-150 / Epistle of Barnabas c.70-130 / Basilides c.130 / The Ophites	Papias c.130-140 / Shepherd of Hermas c.120-140 / Justin Martyr c.150-155 / Irenaeus c.130-202 / Marcion c.140 / Valentinus c.140 / Old Latin Version / Old Syriac Version / Muratorian Canon c.170 / Tatian The Diatessaron c.170	Clement of Alexandria c.150-215 / Tartullian c.150-220 / Origen c.185-254 / Barococcio Canon c.206 / Cyril of Jerusalem c.315-386 / Eusebius c.325-340 / Jerome c.340-420 / Augustine c.400
Matt.	X X X X X X	X X X O X O O O O	X X X O O O O O
Mark	X X X	X X X O O O O O	X X X O O O O O
Luke	X X X X	X O X X O O O	X X X O O O O O
John	X X X X X	X O O X O O O O	X X X O O O O O
Acts	X	X X O O O O	X X X O O O O O
Rom.	X X X	X O X X O O O	O X X O O O O O
1 Cor.	O X X X	X X O X X O O O	O X X O O O O O
2 Cor.	X X X	X X O X O O O	O X X O O O O O
Gal.	X X	X O X O O O	O X X O O O O O
Eph.	X O X X X X	X O X O O O O	X X X O O O O O
Phil.	X X	x O X O O O	O X X O O O O O
Col.	X X X	X O X O O O	O X X O O O O O
1 Thess.	X X	X X O O O O	X X X O O O O O
2 Thess.	X X	X O X O O O	X X X O O O O O
1 Tim.	X X X X	X O O O	O X X O O O O O
2 Tim.	X X	X X O O O	X X X O O O O O
Titus	X X	X X O O O	O X X O O O O O
Philemon	X	X O O O	O O O O O
Hebrews	X X X	X X X X O	O X ? O O O O O
James	X	X O	O O & O O
1 Peter	X X X	X X O O	O X O O O O O O
2 Peter	X X X		? O O ? O O
1 John	X	X X O X X O O O	O X O O O O O
2 John		X O O	? O O ? O O
3 John		O O	? O O ? O O
Jude		O O	X O O ? O O
Revelation	X	O X X O O O	O X O O O O

Fig. 3

This diagram was adapted and modified from Norman L. Geisler and William E. Nix, *A General Introduction to the Bible*. Chicago: Moody Press, 1968, p. 193.

Chapter 7

How Has God Preserved His Word?

In chapter 3 we saw that one of the external evidences demonstrating the Bible to be the Word of God is the miracle of its preservation these 3400 years since Moses began to write before 1400 B.C. The fact of preservation by itself is miraculous enough, but when one adds to this the fact that it has been the target of diabolical hatred and efforts to get rid of it such as no other writing has ever encountered, the hand of God in preserving it for us becomes very plain indeed.

There are three basic ways in which Satan has endeavored to keep the Word of God from men—by destruction, by neglect, and by ignorance. In the Bible itself we find an example of each of these efforts.

From Destruction

Intellectual (Genesis 3:1-6). This is Satan's oldest and most successful method of destroying God's Word in the hearts of men. In the Garden of Eden he used intellectual doubt as the wedge that led Eve into sin. "Hath God said?" has been his favorite tactic through all the ages since. Doubts have been planted in men's minds that have time and again betrayed them into rejecting part or all of God's Word. It lay behind Pharaoh's refusals to heed Moses' demands that he let Israel go free. It lay behind the questioning of Moses' authority in the wilderness. It lay behind Ahab's rejection of Elijah. All the prophets, in fact, were in their own time rejected by many, and were often hounded and even killed because they dared to insist that they spoke the words of God.

Nor has the questioning of God's Word ceased today. It may be an outright denial of the fact that He has spoken to forbid such acts as are practiced by abortionists and homosexuals, or it may be a claim to reinterpret His words and play down His authority and inspiration, as is practiced by the modern liberals. They all are still equally seduced by the age-old question, "Hath God said?"

The very virulence of the attacks made on the Scriptures are themselves testimony to its power as the Word of God. If men really believed this Book to be a mere ancient manuscript as non-authoritative and imperfect as they claim it to be, would they waste their lives in attacking it so violently and persistently? One wonders, for example, if Madalyn Murray O'Hair would give such single-minded devotion to the eradication of God and His Word if she did not actually fear them.

Physical (Jeremiah 36:1-32). Doubting God's Word intellectually often leads not only to rejecting it personally but to destroying it physically. Because the Lord always has His faithful hearers who do believe and practice and proclaim His Word in the face of every intellectual barrage, Satan has from time to time attempted the tactic of literally annihilating God's Word. The prophet Jeremiah records one such early effort tried by King Jehoiakim.

The Lord had commanded Jeremiah to write on a scroll His condemnation of Judah's sinful apostasy and His determination to punish them by giving victory to their powerful enemies, the Babylonians. King Jehoiakim and his advisers considered the prophet's words treasonous and intended to break down the morale of the people in the face of a Babylonian attack. Nevertheless, some powerful princes who heard Jeremiah's secretary, Baruch, reading the scroll in the temple court recognized its power and arranged for it to be read before the king. So infuriated was Jehoiakim by God's message that as each column of the scroll was read he slashed it off with his penknife and tossed it into the fire.

Not so easily, however, is truth destroyed. God commanded Jeremiah to rewrite the scroll and add to it further words that He would give, including an account of the king's action and God's judgment on it. So now, 2500 years later, we can still read and profit by the Word of God that a king's knife and his fire could not destroy.

Satan, however, has not abandoned the tactic. Roman emperors not only persecuted Christians, but they made bonfires of the Scriptures. Efforts to confiscate and destroy the Scriptures translated into the languages of the common people were made even by church dignitaries before and during the Reformation. For example, when William Tyndale's Testaments were being smuggled into England, the Bishop of London bought up and destroyed every copy he could lay hands on—thus supplying funds for even larger printings.[1]

A more modern example comes from the mid-nineteenth century. After missionaries to Madegascar had planted a church and were translating the Bible into the language of the people, an evil queen came to the throne who wanted to re-establish the old ways and stamp out Christianity. She ordered all Bibles hunted out and destroyed, pronouncing dire penalties on the owners. The heroic stories that came out of that bloody time of the efforts of the Christians to protect the Word of God deserve much greater place than they have received in the annals of the martyrs. One noble pastor hid with a copy of Scripture in a cave for two solid years, reading and re-reading his precious Book and depending entirely on his congregation to brave the queen's wrath by bringing him food in the dead of night. In other communities the Bible was hidden in the house set aside for those stricken with contagious diseases—the one place the queen's soldiers dared not search.[2]

In our own day too, totalitarian governments seek to destroy and otherwise ban copies of Scripture. But destruction is no more successful for today's tyrants than it was for Jehoiakim.

The Lord always has His people who will hide it, memorize it, and protect it with their lives. Neither physical nor intellectual force can destroy the Word of God.

From Neglect (2 Kings 21:1-16)

The devil has probably been more successful in seeing God's Word lost through neglect of its use than through destruction by enemies. Judah was guilty of such neglect and thus lost their law for perhaps half a century.

The wicked king Manasseh was at least partly responsible. He had the longest reign of any king of Judah—55 years—and he probably did the most evil. He was enamored by the powerful Assyrians who not long before (in his father's day, in fact) had destroyed the northern kingdom of Israel. He sought to emulate their ways, including their pagan religious rites. As the king went, so went the people, including the priests. Some, no doubt, chose to do what was popular with the king, and others followed reluctantly because they feared his reprisals. Jewish tradition has it that the prophet Isaiah was silenced by Manasseh, who had him sawn asunder.[3]

Two years after Manasseh's death, his grandson Josiah ascended the throne and determined to follow the Lord. He began by ordering the priests to repair the long neglected temple and make it fit again for the worship of Jehovah. In the course of their work, the priests found a copy of the Torah, and for the first time in his life the young king heard the laws of God. As a result, he led the nation in one of its greatest revivals.

From time to time we read of professors, usually those who teach literature, giving their high school or college students a test of basic Bible knowledge to ascertain whether they understand the many biblical allusions scattered through their literature. The results are usually dismal, even among students whose home and church backgrounds are Christian.

This is a serious form of neglect. Christians who would not think of abetting the devil by helping to destroy God's Word, too often play into His hands by neglecting it. We need continually to seek the Lord's power that we may preserve our Bibles from loss by neglect.

From Ignorance (Nehemiah 8:1-8)

Another successful method of Satan is to destroy the effectiveness of the Scripture by keeping people in ignorance of it. An excellent example of this problem and how it was overcome is found in the Book of Nehemiah. You remember the setting. After the close of the long Babylonian Captivity, the Persian king Artaxerxes had appointed Nehemiah, his cupbearer, governor of Judah and supplied him with a bodyguard and permission to rebuild Jerusalem. After rebuilding the walls, Nehemiah devoted himself to routing ungodliness from the land and making the life-style of the law of Moses the norm for the people.

One major roadblock to his efforts was the fact that during the long years of the captivity many of the people had forgotten their native Hebrew tongue and spoke instead in Aramaic, the *lingua franca* of the Persian Empire. Thus the Hebrew Scriptures became a closed book to them. Younger ones had grown up largely in ignorance of its teachings. To counteract this ignorance, Nehemiah and Ezra, his co-worker, chose to call all the people together to hear the law read. The reading took an entire morning (The congregation stood all that time!). To insure understanding, the governor brought together a number of men skilled in translation. As Ezra read, these men translated and interpreted the Hebrew. In the words of Nehemiah, they "gave the sense, and caused them to understand the reading."

That the effort was successful is demonstrated in the remainder of the chapter which shows that they first grieved because they had fallen so far short of God's law, then rejoiced because they could read and understand the Scripture and finally put into practice the commands of the law.

Throughout the history of the church the Holy Spirit has raised up translators and interpreters to combat the satanic efforts to keep men in ignorance of God's Word. Even in the earliest centuries of Christendom there were versions of

Scripture in Latin, Aramaic, Syriac and Gothic. After Constantine, however, as the church became a powerful hierarchy, it decreed that only its priests were competent to handle the Scriptures, that Latin (though itself only a translation of the original Hebrew and Greek) was the sacred language in which the Word must be housed, and that the average man should not attempt to read or interpret it for himself. In time the lower ranks of priests became as ignorant as their parishioners because their training was less and less from Scripture and more and more from traditions of the church. And so the blind led the blind into deeper darkness while corruption increased in the church.

There was always opposition to this policy. Church history is dotted with heroic stories of men and groups of believers separated from the mainstream church who made copies of Scripture in their native tongues and sought to share it with others. In his book about missions during the Middle Ages, Raymond Edman appropriately calls his chapter on these scattered believers "Candle Lights."[4] With the invention of the printing press, however, and the acceptance of the Reformation teaching that Scripture alone is our authority for faith and practice, and that every Christian is a priest capable of understanding it under the guidance of the Holy Spirit, translations into all the common tongues of Europe proliferated.

The church fought hard against this threat to her authority, and some of the translators became martyrs. One of these was William Tyndale, mentioned above. He was the outstanding translator of the Bible into English. Tyndale once retorted to a church dignitary who opposed him that he hoped his work would result in enabling the boy who drove the plough to understand more of the Scripture than did the learned bishop.[5]

Tyndale was hounded out of England and continued his labors in Geneva from whence his English translations were smuggled back into England. Betrayed by a trusted associate, he was tried as a heretic and burned at the stake in 1534. His dying words were a prayer, "Lord, open the king of England's eyes." Only two years later, Henry VIII ordered that a copy of the

Scriptures in the English language be placed in every pulpit in his realm and regularly read to the people. The Bible authorized for that placement was the Matthew Bible, which contained the work of Tyndale. Thus Tyndale's New Testament, which Henry had proscribed in 1525, was authorized under another name in 1536.[6]

Bible translation has been a priority of modern missionary strategy beginning with William Carey, who spent much of his career translating the Bible into several of the native tongues of India. Missions have recognized that to build a strong indigenous church capable of remaining solid and experiencing growth even if missionary support should be withdrawn, requires that the people have the Scripture in the language they best understand. The church in Madagascar, previously mentioned, is an example of this, and the story of how they got their translation is one of the more fascinating but lesser known in the annals of Bible translation.

The evil queen of Madagascar had ordered all missionaries deported just as their work had begun to bear fruit. About that time, however, she had been presented with some soap by a British ambassador and became enamored with it. As a result she agreed to delay the deportation of the missionaries if they would work out a formula for soap made from native materials and teach her workmen to manufacture it. One man among the missionaries had studied a little chemistry and he was delegated to find the formula and teach the apprentices. The others would work feverishly day and night to complete their translation of the Bible into the Malagasy language before their time ran out. The real challenge was to show enough success in the soap enterprise to keep the queen encouraged, but not enough for her to decide her workmen could go ahead on their own. So well did he succeed in walking such a tightrope that at the same time as her patience was exhausted, the finished translation was put into the hands of trusted converts. The result was a church which grew manyfold even during her twenty year reign of terror.[7]

Ignorance of God's Word is usually the child of neglect. The children of neglectful Christians are apt to be ignorant Christians, and their children not Christians at all. So subtly we can become allies of Satan in his efforts to destroy the Word of God. It is with good reason that in the law Moses commanded parents to constantly teach their children God's Word "when thou sittest in thine house, and when thou walkest by the way, and when thou liest down, and when thou risest up."[8] Thus we and they can become God's servants in preserving His Word from destruction.

SUMMARY

The story of the preservation of the Scripture is one of a multitude of miracles against satanic odds. The struggle to discredit and eradicate the Word of God began in the Garden of Eden and continues today. The three main tactics used against it are destruction—both intellectual and physical, neglect, and ignorance. All three methods were used in Bible times and are still being used today.

The struggle is not over. The battle is waged today by scholars who defend its intellectual integrity, by a vast army of missionary translators who disseminate it to ever new groups of people, and by conscientious parents and teachers who are determined that knowledge of it will not die with their generation.

FOOTNOTES

[1]Maurice A. Price, *The Ancestry of our English Bible*, 3rd rev. ed. New York: Harper & Brothers, 1956, p. 247.
[2]T. T. Matthews, *Thirty Years in Madegascar*. London: Religious Tract Society, 1904.
[3]See Heb. 11:37; cf. also 2 Kings 21:16 and 2 Chron. 33:9-10.
[4]*The Light in Dark Ages*. Wheaton, Ill.: Van Kampen Press, 1949.
[5]Price, *Op. cit.*, p. 244.
[6]*Ibid.*, pp. 250, 255.
[7]Matthews, *Op. cit.*
[8]Deut. 6:7

Chapter 8

Do We Really Have The Scripture That God Inspired?

Transmission and Textual Criticism

> We believe that the Holy Bible was written by men divinely inspired, and is a perfect treasure of heavenly instruction; that it has God for its author, salvation for its end, and truth without any mixture of error for its matter, that it reveals the principles by which God will judge us; and therefore is, and shall remain to the end of the world, the true centre of Christian union, and the supreme standard by which all human conduct, creeds, and opinions should be tried.[1]

This creedal statement, written in 1833, was widely accepted among Baptist groups and was an accurate expression of the faith of many other evangelical bodies. What it says is still the faith of the fundamental churches and the many evangelical organizations which serve them, but they have worded their doctrinal statements in a conscious effort to avoid any misunderstanding or misinterpretation of what they believe. The following is typical:

> We believe the Holy Scriptures of the Old and New Testaments to be the verbally inspired word of God, the final authority for faith and life, inerrant in the original writings, infallible and God-breathed (2 Timothy 3:16,17; 2 Peter 1:20. 21; Matthew 5:18; John 16:12,13).[2]

Interestingly enough, earlier statements of faith show entirely different emphases. The post-Reformation documents, such as the Westminster Confession of Faith and the Thirty-nine Articles of the Anglican Church, stress that Scripture is the sole rule of faith and life, and list the books to be accepted as canonical, so as to exclude the Apocrypha. Both these emphases, of course, were in opposition to Roman Catholic teaching.

Going further back in history, the early creeds, such as the Apostles' Creed, did not even include a statement about the Scriptures. It is only in comparatively recent times it has become necessary to spell out one's belief concerning the Scriptures as an article of faith.

Having confessed our faith, however, in the verbal inspiration of the Scripture, we are still faced with the question, What does that really mean? How do you know the Bible you are reading is the same as the original Hebrew and Greek autographs?[3]

When we pick up a book written in the last five hundred years, we have no doubt that the words we read are the very words the author wrote. The invention of the printing press, about 1450, was probably the most important invention for the art of communication since the alphabet. It made possible the publishing of thousands of identical copies once the press had been set up accurately. The first printed book was the Latin Bible. The New Testament was first published in Greek by Erasmus, in 1516 in Basel. The Hebrew Old Testament was also first published in 1516, in Venice. Each depended upon a manuscript[4] tradition that is important to understand if we are to appreciate the authority and accuracy of our English Bibles.

The Transmission of the Old Testament Text (Matthew 5:18)

God gave us His revelation because He wanted us to believe it and live by it. He did not inspire it and then leave it to its fate at the hands of careless or antagonistic men. Speaking of the Old Testament Scriptures, Jesus assured us that "Till

Do We Really Have The Scripture That God Inspired?

heaven and earth pass, one jot or one tittle shall in no wise pass from the law, till all be fulfilled." The jot is the *yod*, or smallest letter of the Hebrew alphabet. It looks like a comma placed above the line. The tittle is the tiny mark that is sometimes all that distinguished one Hebrew letter from another (see fig.4).

In the three thousand years that intervened between Moses and the invention of the printing press, during which time all copying of books had to be done by hand, how was the correct text maintained?

The Masoretic Text. Aside from a few isolated fragments, the oldest witness to the text of the Hebrew Old Testament before the discovery of the Dead Sea Scrolls in 1947, was dated in the tenth or eleventh century—or almost a millennium and a half after the Old Testament Canon was completed (probably in Ezra's day). Early in Jewish history Jewish scribes realized the problem and importance of preserving an accurate text.

Now anyone who has ever attempted to copy a lengthy text is aware of how easy it is to make a mistake—a careless spelling, skipping a few words or a line because the eye picks up a word repeated a little further along, writing a familiar text from a slightly faulty memory, etc. Thus, very early, the scribes began to set up careful rules which anyone who attempted to copy Scripture must follow unfailingly. Over a period of time seventeen of these rules were developed. They specified the kind of materials for writing and required meticulous care in copying. For example, the name of God must not be written with a newly dipped pen; this guarded against a blot of ink marring it. Limits were set on the number of lines to a column and the number of letters in a line. The letters were actually counted to make sure not one was left out. If more than a certain number of errors were found in a text, it could not be read in the synagogue. Usually it would be destroyed.

When treasured manuscripts were worn and in danger of leading a copyist to make errors, they were given a respectful burial. Either they were actually buried underground, or they were put into a tomb-like compartment called a *genizah*, there never to be read again. A *genizah* in a Cairo synagogue has produced for us some of the oldest examples of the Masoretic text.

We now know that originally in Old Testament times vowels were not written, and that generally Hebrew and other Semitic languages could be written and understood without vowel letters. At first scribes began to use certain weak consonants like y, w, h and aleph (which has become our A) to indicate vowels. This had taken place before the time of the Dead Sea Scrolls.

From the fifth to the tenth centuries A.D. there flourished a group of Jewish scholars known as the Masoretes. Their contribution was to record by means of dots and dashes above and below the line of consonants the vowels that indicated how the Hebrew words were pronounced in their day. It has been suggested that this above and below placement was made to avoid disobeying Moses' command against adding or subtracting from his commands.[5] The Masoretes also added marginal notes that urged others to "read" differently than they wrote. Thus, although they refused to change the text, they recorded how a difficult phrase was understood in their day.

Other scribal notes indicated which word of a book was the middle one, which was the middle between the first and middle, and so forth. Thus a copyist had additional checks for revealing any mistakes in his manuscript.

All these safeguards give us some indication of the great care with which the scribes circumscribed the transmission of the sacred text. Thus the Hebrew text published in 1516 was the only known text, even though the survival of the Samaritan text of the Pentateuch and the Greek text of the Septuagint gave hints that in ancient times there might have been rival texts. In fact, the Talmud records a tradition that three texts of the law were preserved in the Temple before its destruction in A.D. 70.[6]

The Dead Sea Scrolls. The discovery of the Dead Sea Scrolls, beginning in 1947, brought to light the first positive evidence we had of there being various texts in Hebrew. At the same

Do We Really Have The Scripture That God Inspired? 75

time they also revealed with what great care the Masoretic text had been handed down. Despite evidence of some very minor scribal errors, the traditional text was found to predominate. Thus the Masoretic text was found to exist and to be the preferred (that is, the most frequently found) text in the first century A.D.

Between 1947 and 1956, eleven caves were discovered in the vicinity of the Wadi Qumran. Tens of thousands of manuscript fragments were recovered. Evidence of almost four hundred different scrolls were found. All the Old Testament books except Esther are represented, some by twelve to fifteen different scrolls. The favorite books seem to have been Deuteronomy, Isaiah and Psalms. It was further noted that much greater care was taken in copying and handling the canonical books than was the case with other scrolls less sacred. All these scrolls must have been hidden in the caves before the fall of Jerusalem in A.D. 70. Further south, along the Wadi Murabba'at, several more caves were discovered which contained manuscripts that must date before the Jewish revolt of A.D. 132-135.

An interesting development of these Dead Sea manuscripts was the discovery of a Hebrew text tradition which could be the source of the Greek Septuagint.[7] Since the Septuagint was widely used by the early church, and its form of the Messianic prophecies was particularly agreeable to Christian teaching, this text tradition was apparently rejected and thus not preserved by later Jewish scholars after the fall of Jerusalem. No evidence of any other text than the tratitional Masoretic was found at Wadi Murabba'at.

A third text tradition of the Pentateuch found among the Dead Sea Scrolls resembles the Samaritan Pentateuch.[8] We thus have support for the Talmud tradition that before the destruction of the temple there existed three texts of the law.

These discoveries are further attestation of the desire of the scribes and Jewish leaders not to add or remove anything in the Scriptures they possessed. Even though these three manuscript traditions had minor differences, they refused to change any of them but preserved all three. From recent archaeological discoveries, then, we have unique evidence of the antiquity and reliability of the Old Testament text from which our English translations are derived.

The Transmission of the New Testament Text (I Peter 1:24-25)

When Peter spoke of the Word of the Lord enduring forever, he was quoting from Psalm 119:89. Thus in both the Old and New Testaments we have direct assurance, inspired by the Holy Spirit to David and to Peter, that none of His Word—Old or New Testaments—should ever be lost.

The New Testament manuscripts. Geisler and Nix have pointed out:

> The integrity of the Old Testament text was established primarily by the fidelity of the transmisson process which was later confirmed by the Dead Sea Scrolls. The fidelity of the New Testament text, however, rests in the multiplicity of the extant manuscripts. Whereas the Old Testament had only a few complete manuscripts, all of which were good as the result of ancient rabbinical textual work, the New Testament has more copies—although of poorer quality (more variants)—which enable the present-day textual critic to establish the true text.[9]

In other words, what is lost in the quality of the New Testament manuscripts is made up in the quantity. The richness of the sources for the Greek New Testament is the envy of all other ancient studies. Nearly five thousand manuscripts are known and more are being discovered all the time. The careful study of these, comparing their different readings, determines what the original autographs of the apostles must have contained.

How does this compare with other ancient manuscripts? F. F. Bruce explains:

> Perhaps we can appreciate how wealthy the New Testament is in manuscript attestation if we compare the textual material for other ancient historical works. For Caesar's *Gallic War* (composed between 58 and 50 B.C.) there are several extant MSS, but only nine or ten are good, and the oldest is some 900 years later than Caesar's day. Of the 142 books of the Roman History of

Do We Really Have The Scripture That God Inspired? 77

Livy (50 B.C.—A.D. 17) only 35 survive; these are known to us from not more than twenty MSS of any consequence, only one of which, and that containing fragments of Books iii-vi, is as old as the fourth century. Of the fourteen books of the *Histories* of Tacitus (c. A.D. 100) only four and a half survive; of the sixteen books of his *Annals*, ten survive in full and two in part. The text of these extant portions of his two great historical works depends entirely on two MSS, one of the ninth century and one of the eleventh. The extant MSS of his minor works (*Dialogue de Oratoribus, Agricola, Germania*) all descend from a codex of the tenth century. The History of Thucydides (c. 460-400 A.C.) is known to us from eight MSS, the earliest belonging to about the beginning of the Christian era. The same is true of the history of Herodotus (c. 480-425 B.C.). Yet no classical scholar would listen to an argument that the authenticity of Herodotus or Thucydides is in doubt because the earliest MSS of their works which are of any use to us are over 1,300 years later than the originals.[10]

Research into old monastery archives and archaeological discoveries have turned up an impressive array of very ancient texts. In the Vatican library was found the Codex Vaticanus, dated 325-350 A.D. In St. Catherine's monastery on the slope of Mount Sinai was found the Codex Sinaiticus, also dated to the fourth century. Both contain nearly the whole Bible (the Old Testament in Greek). From the sands of Egypt, caves, and other places have come seventy-nine manuscripts on papyrus. The Chester Beatty papyri are dated to the third century, or about two hundred years after the autographs were written, and they include most of the New Testament. The oldest undisputed manuscript is a fragment of John dated about A.D. 135, or less than half a century after the autograph. In the early 1970s Father O'Callahan, a Spanish Jesuit, while pondering some unidentified fragments of Greek manuscripts found in a Dead Sea cave, came up with an identification of the text with the gospel of Mark. Now, nearly ten years later, no one has been able to produce a better identification. From this breakthrough, O'Callahan went on to identify others and as a result claims to have identified fragments of four portions of

Mark and one each of Acts, Romans, 1 Timothy, James and 2 Peter. Although there is still no general acceptance of his work, Estrada and White have produced a strong argument in support of his results.[11]

The problem of scribal errors. The fact that we admit scribal errors have crept into the text has often confused people into thinking that our English New Testament is based on a faulty text. In 1952 when the Revised Standard Version first appeared, a magazine article for popular consumption said that there are "probably 50,000 errors" in our New Testament.[12] Others have suggested that there are up to 200,000 variants (errors) in the New Testament. Quoted blandly as they were in *Look*, such figures convey the impression that the New Testament is a totally unreliable text and that in relying on it for assurance of having the Word of God for our lives and eternal destiny, we are leaning on a bruised reed.

NOT SO! When we understand what is meant by these statistics, we realize they are a powerful argument for the integrity of the text. If one particular word is misspelled in two thousand manuscripts, it is counted as two thousand errors, even though we may well know the correct spelling and have it attested by three thousand manuscripts. In fact, it is suggested that the 200,000 errors represent only 10,000 places in the text where these variants occur. But even this, though it may sound staggering, is not so remarkable when we realize that the whole New Testament is in consideration. The New Testament text has been calculated to be actually 99.5 percent pure. And nothing in even this minute variance touches a basic teaching.

In short, we can say that, except for certain disputed passages, most of which were noted in our Scofield Bibles half a century ago, we have preserved for us actually what the apostles wrote 1900 years ago. And this despite the fact that for 1300 years the transmission of the text depended on hand copies made by scribes who all too often made errors—

Do We Really Have The Scripture That God Inspired?

sometimes even deliberate ones—but which we can correct on the basis of the study of thousands of manuscripts.

The study of these manuscripts is called the science of textual criticism. By this method spelling errors are quickly corrected. Of more serious weight are words or phrases that if changed to suit one manuscript would seriously affect the sense. Beyond this is a small group of verses whose authenticity is in doubt because they are missing in many of the better ancient sources. The chief of these are the ending to Mark (Mark 16:9-20), the woman taken in adultery (John 7:53—8:11), John 5:4b, and 1 John 5:7.

On the basis of the particular scribal errors found in them, manuscripts are placed in families possessing the same combination of these, then each family is in turn evaluated until we arrive at a reasonable solution as to the original text.

How does this compare with other ancient documents that have come down to us? The *Iliad* of Homer certainly did not have the status of Scripture to the Greeks, but it did describe what was believed about their gods. Its popularity is attested by the fact that 643 manuscripts have survived. Yet the difference in the area of doubtful readings is striking. While it has been estimated that forty lines of the New Testament out of 20,000 are in doubt, the *Illiad*, which is only 15,600 lines long, has 764 lines in doubt. The same may be said for the *Mahabharata* of India, which indeed is regarded as Scripture by many Hindus. Of 250,000 lines about ten percent, or 26,000, are in doubt through textual corruption. The actual lines in doubt in the New Testament amount to only .5 percent. In other words, our present text is actually about 99.5 percent pure. And, let it be re-emphasized, that .5 percent does not affect any basic doctrine.

Thus, although we do not possess an autograph of any New Testament book, we can with assurance use it, believing we possess the actual words of the apostles as inspired by the Holy Spirit, as accurately as they can be translated into English.

Certainly—as cannot be stressed often enough—no major doctrine of Christianity stands in jeopardy because a text referring to it is in doubt. The only warning this study gives us is that we must not attempt to construct some new doctrine or issue on some single obscure test.

We can read our Bibles—both Old and New Testaments—as God's actual words to us.

SUMMARY

From the time that Moses first began to put God's Word in writing until the invention of the printing press, a period of about three thousand years, all copies of the Scriptures had to be made by hand. In spite of this, the Holy Spirit has so overseen and preserved His Word that we need have no doubt that the Bibles we read today are virtually the words that the prophets and apostles originally wrote down.

The Old Testament text is guaranteed by the extreme care which the scribes took to assure that not "one jot or one tittle" should in any way be altered. The New Testament text is attested by the great abundance of manuscripts which can be compared one against the other, with variants traced to their source, and by the insignificance of such scribal variations.

Our statements of faith affirm that the Old and New Testaments are inspired of God and are inerrant in the original writings. We may safely add that to all intents and purposes we have those writings today.

FOOTNOTES

[1] The New Hampshire Confession of Faith, Article I. Taken from Philip Schaff, *The Creeds of Christendom*, Vol. III, *Evangelical Creeds.* New York: Harper & Brothers, 1919, p. 742.

[2] From Articles of Faith of the Independent Fundamantal Churches of America.

[3] By autograph, we refer to the original manuscript of the prophet or apostle as written by himself or his secretary (amanuensis).

Do We Really Have The Scripture That God Inspired? 81

⁴"A manuscript is a handwritten literary composition in contrast to a printed copy." Norman L. Geisler and William E. Nix, *A General Introduction to the Bible*. Chicago: Moody Press, 1968, p. 267.

⁵See Deut. 4:2; 12:32.

⁶William Chomsky, *Hebrew: The Eternal Language*. Philadelphia: The Jewish Publication Society of America, 1957, p. 144.

⁷The word "Septuagint" literally means "seventy," and is often abbreviated to LXX. It was a Greek translation made from the Hebrew in Alexandria, Egypt, about 200 B.C. for the royal library there. Tradition says it was the work of seventy scholars, hence its name.

⁸The Samaritans (rejected by Nehemiah because of their mixed blood—see Nehemiah 13:3 and Ezra 4:2-3) treasure a copy of the five books of Moses they believe was brought to them by a son of the high priest in Jerusalem who would not leave his non-Jewish wife as Nehemiah demanded (Nehemiah 13:28). The major difference between this copy of the Torah and the Masoretic text is that it justifies worship on Mount Gerizim instead of in Jerusalem (cf. John 4:20).

⁹Geisler and Nix, *Op. cit.*, p. 267.

¹⁰F. F. Bruce, *Are the New Testament Documents Reliable?* Grand Rapids: Wm. B. Eerdmans Publishing Company, 1954, p. 20.

¹¹David Estrada and William White, Jr., *The First New Testament*. Nashville: Thomas Nelson, Inc., 1978.

¹²Hartzel Spence, *Look* Magazine, Feb. 26, 1952.

The Tittle

ר = R   ופ = D   ב = B   כ = K

Fig. 4

Chapter 9

How Has The Bible Come Into English?

The story of how God's Word was made available to us in our English tongue is as full of excitement and drama as can be found anywhere in the long history of the church.

Forerunners of the English Bible (2 Timothy 2:1-2)

In his last message to his beloved son in the Lord, Paul instructed Timothy to commit the transmission of the gospel into the hands of "faithful men." It was a succession of such faithful men who brought the Bible to England. There are traditions that Christianity reached England in the days of the apostles. Certainly it was there by the second century, although our first positive record is of the presence of three English bishops at the Council of Arles in 314 A.D. Since England was at that time an outpost of the Roman Empire, the church there would have had the Latin Scriptures. There is no suggestion of any native version.

Early English versions. In the fifth century the Anglo-Saxons invaded Britain, pushing the native Celts back into Wales, Ireland and Scotland. One of these British Celts was St. Patrick who took Christianity to Ireland. Meanwhile, St. Augustine of Canterbury re-introduced Christianity to Britain in 597 A.D. and at the same time imposed on them for the first time allegiance to the pope in Rome.

The first faithful man of whom we have any record who brought the Scriptures into Anglo-Saxon was a poor cowherd named Caedmon who lived about 680 A.D. He was so shy that when he attended parties where each guest was expected to entertain in song, he would slip out before his turn came. On one such occasion he hid in a stable and fell asleep. As he dreamed, he heard someone say, "Caedmon, sing me a song."

"I don't know how," he protested. "That is why I left the feast."

"But you shall sing to me," insisted the voice.

"What shall I sing?" he asked. The reply was, "Sing about the creation of all things." Immediately he began to sing of the glory of the Creator.

Before long it was recognized that Caedmon had a God-given gift to sing the Scripture in his native tongue. He was persuaded to join the monastery where he had kept the cattle. For the rest of his life he learned Bible passages and turned them into Anglo-Saxon poems. [Thus Caedmon was the first English paraphraser.] Although these poems were not translations they were received joyfully by the peasants who heard only Latin in church and did not understand it.

We know about Caedmon only because the Venerable Bede (673-735) preserved his story in the history he wrote of the church in Britain down to his own day.[1] Bede was a scholar determined to translate the gospel of John into Anglo-Saxon. Expecting death, he used an assistant to write quickly as he dictated. At last the lad cried, "It is finished, master."

"Truly, it is finished," Bede replied. And he died singing the doxology.

The next faithful man was a king—Alfred the Great (870-906). He, too, was a scholar interested in having the Scriptures in Anglo-Saxon. He had the Ten Commandments placed at the head of his law code. He also sponsored a translation of the Psalms, but no copy of it has survived.

Stephen Langton, a doctor in the University of Paris and later Archbishop of Canterbury, made an important contribution about 1228 A.D. He introduced the divisions we know as chapters. Although he used the Latin version, his chapters have become standard in all Catholic and Protestant Bibles.

The first English translation. Compare these three renditions of the beginning of the Lord's prayer:

Uren Fader dhic art in hoefnas (Anglo-Saxon, 870)
Our Fadir that art in houenes (Wycliffe, 1382)
Our father which arte in heven (Tyndale, 1525)

As you can see, Anglo-Saxon is not so much English as it is a forerunner of English. It is at least equally as close to German. The first genuinely English translation was made in the late fourteenth century by one of the greatest of our faithful men, John Wycliffe (1320-1384). Although he was a priest, he abhorred the greed and crafty deceit that so many others of his profession routinely practiced on the laity. He believed that the people's best protection against being so misused was in their ability to read the Bible for themselves. He was the first to translate the whole Bible into English. It was a tremendous work and earned him the undying hatred of church leaders. They dared not make him a martyr because his patron was John of Gaunt, son of Edward III, and a powerful man at court, but years after his death the hierarchy had his bones disinterred and burned. A Wycliffe Bible is a rare treasure today, so assiduously were they hunted down and burned.

Although Wycliffe's Bible may have been a translation of a translation (the Latin Vulgate), it was nevertheless a great step in bringing the Scriptures to the common man. Since the printing press had not been invented, all copies were hand written and thus expensive. It is said that poor men gladly gave a load of hay for a copy of a single Psalm, or a day's work for a few chapters. Wycliffe's Bibles and his doctrines were disseminated throughout England by his itinerant disciples, called Lollards, thus laying the foundation for the break with Rome a century later. Wycliffe has been called "the morning star of the Reformation."

The Reformation Translations

It was the invention of the printing press about 1450 that

made possible the cheap and widespread dissemination of the teachings of men like Luther as well as of translations, thus bringing about a successful Reformation.

The first printed English Bible. The sixteenth century saw a number of faithful men work on English translations, using the newly available printed Bibles in Hebrew and Greek to translate from the original tongues. The first of these, and the one whose career makes the most exciting reading, was William Tyndale (1484-1535), who was reportedly skilled in seven languages (Hebrew, Greek, Latin, Italian, Spanish, French and, of course, English). As for the quality of his English, it suffices to say that our King James Version frequently follows his renderings.

With single-minded purpose Tyndale devoted his life to translating the Scriptures into English. By 1525 his New Testament was ready for publication. The Bishop of London was so incensed that he bought up all he could in order to burn them. John Foxe reports that when Sir Thomas More asked a Tyndale supporter how his master got the means to produce so many New Testaments, the man replied, "My Lord, I will tell you truly: it is the Bishop of London that hath holpen us, for he hath bestowed among us a great deal of money upon New Testaments to burn and that hath been, and yet is, our only succor and comfort."[2]

Tyndale succeeded in translating from the Hebrew only through 2 Chronicles before his enemies caught up with him and had him tried for heresy and burned at the stake. Even as he uttered his dying prayer, "Lord, open the King of England's eyes," Henry VIII was relenting on his opposition to the translation of the Bible into English. Months before Tyndale's death, Miles Coverdale was producing an edition based on Tyndale's English, Zwingli's German, and the Latin Vulgate. Although edited rather than translated, he gets credit for publishing the first complete English printed Bible.

Busy century for translators. The century beginning with Tyndale and culminating in the King James Version was one

How Has The Bible Come Into English?

of many translations. Bible translation had become popular, and although Henry VIII still had no love for Tyndale, he encouraged other men in the work. John Rogers, a disciple of Tyndale who had received his mentor's manuscript of Joshua through 2 Chronicles, produced under the name of Thomas Matthew a Bible that was Tyndale from Genesis to Chronicles, Coverdale for the rest of the Old Testament and Apocrypha, and Tyndale again for the New Testament. He thus preserved Tyndale's work without stirring up his opponents. Henry VIII, who had banned Tyndale's New Testament, authorized this pseudonymous work of Tyndale to be used in the churches.

Thomas Cromwell, a shrewd politician and far-sighted churchman, persuaded Coverdale to undertake a revision that would bring his version closer to the Hebrew and Greek, and hence to Tyndale. In 1539 this appeared and was soon called *The Great Bible*. Ira Price says the result was only a revised Matthew Bible. When Archbishop Cranmer of Canterbury wrote a preface endorsing it, a remarkable turnabout resulted. Price says, "So Bishop Tunstall, who had so vigorously condemned, bought up and burned Tyndale's New Testament, now formally on the title page endorsed its publication and use."[3]

But Bible burning was not a thing of the past. After the brief reign of Henry's successor, the devout but sickly Edward VI (1547-1553), his eldest sister Mary, the Catholic, became queen (1553-1558). She is remembered as Bloody Mary, not only for the number of bishops and others she burned in her short five-year reign, but also for her efforts to hunt down and burn all the thousands of copies of the Great Bible that had been hidden from her spies. Out of this period come heroic stories of ordinary men, women and children protecting their Bibles at tremendous risk. Mary's work had the significant result of driving the scholars out of England into Germany, and especially to Geneva and to Calvin. Coverdale, now a bishop, was among them. Here a new English version was prepared, called the *Geneva Bible*. It soon became the favorite of the reformers in England. This is the version quoted by

Shakespeare, and the version brought by the Puritans to New England.

When Elizabeth I (1558-1603) succeeded her sister on the English throne, the religious situation was again reversed. The Great Bible was brought back to the churches and the queen presided over a compromise between the high church Rome-leaning faction on the right and the Calvin-style Puritans on the left. Although the Geneva Bible was by now the most popular among English Protestants, its polemical anti-Catholic explanatory notes in the margins made it unacceptable to the compromisers. A new version was therefore authorized with directions to follow the Great Bible except where "it varieth manifestly" from the Greek and Hebrew. The result was called the *Bishops' Bible*. It was published without notes and retained a great deal of Tyndale, although in the New Testament the Geneva Bible readings were often preferred.

Although there were lesser translations and many revisions of these versions, there was one other really important one during this century. Just as Mary had driven out the Reformers, so Elizabeth drove out the Catholic papal supporters. The scholars among them founded an English college at Douai, Flanders. Feeling a need to meet the Reformers on their own ground, they produced a Catholic version full of notes justifying Catholic doctrine. The Rheims-Douai Version of 1609-10 was the result. Since the Council of Trent had canonized the Latin Vulgate, the Douai Version is really a translation of a translation, and that rather literally.

The King James Version. The climax of this busy century of translation was the King James Version. When James VI of Scotland ascended the English throne as James I of England, the Puritans thought their time had come. James had been raised a Scottish Presbyterian under the watchful eye of no less a reformer than John Knox. But the king had had his fill of synods and congregational government. He was determined to rule by divine right.

However, as the most learned monarch ever to sit on the

How Has The Bible Come Into English? 89

English throne, he did concede that the Bishop's Bible should be replaced in the churches by a fresh translation. At his command, fifty-four of the finest scholars of the realm were appointed to the work. Only forty-seven names have survived, and we know all those to have been men of piety and scholarship. Fifteen guide rules were agreed upon. The committee divided into three groups, dividing the Bible and Apocrypha among them. Most important of the rules were: that the Bishops' Bible should be followed and "as little altered as the truth of the original will permit"; familiar eccesiastical words would be retained; no marginal notes except for parallel passages. The committee used not only the Greek and Hebrew texts, but consulted such other ancient versions as the Vulgate and Syriac. Price says, "When we consider that the Bishop's Bible was a slightly revised edition of Tyndale's translation, we can appreciate better his far-reaching contribution to the history of the English Bible."[4]

Although in spots the King James Version may be criticized for poor translation, it has on the whole stood the test of time and actually shaped the course of the English language, so that we today speak with an Oxford accent instead of a London cockney accent.

Although for a time advocates of the Geneva Bible resisted the new version, it gradually by virtue of its undeniable excellence triumphed to the point that even today—in the middle of another century of many translations—it survives as the best-loved and most read of all English versions.

SUMMARY

The history of the Bible in English goes back to Anglo-Saxon times. However the first truly English translation was that of John Wycliffe (1320-1384), "the morning star of the Reformation." The translator of most far-reaching influence was William Tyndale (1484-1535). Although he lived at a time of strong sectarian rivalries when every group endorsed a different translation, most of them depended heavily, although without giving him credit, on his work. When James I ended the confusion in 1611 by authorizing the preparation of the King James Version, Tyndale's translation was still the mainstay of its wording.

Even though we are now living in another century of proliferating translations, the King James Version is still the first choice of many evangelical believers.

FOOTNOTES

[1] *Historia ecclesiastica (Ecclesiastical History)*. Bede wrote in Latin, which was the language of all educated people of his day.

[2] *Book of Martyrs*, Philadelphia: John C. Winston Co., 1926, p. 181.

[3] Ira M. Price, *The Ancestry of Our English Bible*, 3rd Rev. Ed. with Wm. A. Irwin. New York: Harper & Brothers, 1956, p. 258.

[4] *Ibid.*, p. 274.

Chapter 10

Which Version Should I Use?

Translations! Translations! Translations! Faced with the overabundance of versions that have been produced within our own lifetime, it is no wonder that many Christians are confused when they must make a choice for themselves. A few years ago Zondervan introduced a publication entitled *The New Testament from 26 Translations*, which prints the King James Version phrase in bold black type, and under each phrase the most important variations culled from twenty-five others. Already this helpful volume needs a major updating. Among recent versions not included are *Today's English Version* (*Good News for Modern Man*) which was first published about the same time and now has millions of copies in print. Nor does it have the *New International Version* which was not then available, but which bids fair to become, at least among evangelicals, the most widely accepted modern translation.

Before discussing the translations, it is well to emphasize that there is no one "best" for every person or every purpose. In this respect, Miles Coverdale, one of the Reformation translators, said:

> Now for thy part, most gentle reader, take in good worth that I here offer thee with a good will, and let this present translation be no prejudice to the other that out of the Greek have been translated afore, or shall be hereafter. For if thou open thine eyes and consider well the gift of the Holy Ghost therein, thou shalt see that *One translation declareth, openeth and illustrateth another, and that in many cases one is a plain commentary unto another.*[1]

Why Do We Still Need Revisions?

One wonders if anyone ever actually made the oft-quoted remark, "If the King James Version was good enough for St. Paul, it is good enough for me." If so, such a one might be shocked at how different in appearance and tone his Bible is from the original edition of 1611. Before it was half a century old corrections were being made in it, and it is still being done.

A large portion of these corrections were mere printer's errors. For example, one printing has become known as the "wicked Bible" because in the seventh commandment the word "not" was inadvertantly omitted. Other changes have modernized the spelling and punctuation and added to the cross references. In 1769, a Dr. Benjamin F. Blaney introduced 65,000 such changes. To insist that the King James text is sacrosanct is to be unaware of its history. The edition of the 1611 translators has undergone almost continual editing. The New Scofield Reference Bible is only the latest in a long line of revisions of the King James Version.[2]

Reasons for a revised version. When the Lord gave the prophet Habbakuk an important message for the people of his generation, He ordered him to "Write the vision and make it plain upon tables that he may run that readeth."[3] As we have sought to stress, God wants His Word to be clearly understood so that its hearers may become prompt and accurate doers. The King James Version was written in the language best understood by the people of its day. (Have you ever noticed that even the peasants in Shakespeare's plays speak King James English?) In fact, the almost universal (in English speaking countries) reverence for and knowledge of the Bible contributed to the language so that the normal processes of change were greatly slowed down. Nevertheless, no language is stagnant, and within three centuries that of 1611 was noticeably archaic and hard to understand by those who had not been reared in its tradition. Thus, by the last third of the nineteenth century many voices clamored for a new revision.

The first and most obvious reason for the growing demand

Which Version Should I Use?

was the change in English usage. Except for the Quakers, no one any longer used the old second person singular of "thee" and "thou" in ordinary speech. Neither did we any longer describe our activities in terms like "asketh," "doeth," "heareth," or "knoweth."

More important is the fact that many English words had undergone a change of meaning in the course of the centuries, some becoming the opposite of what they had been. Almost everyone knows that "charity" earlier meant a self-giving, reaching-out love; today it is alms, no matter how coldly bestowed. A few other examples:

1. Allow (Romans 7:15). Meant *understand* rather than *permit*.

2. By and by (Mark 6:25; Luke 21:9). Meant *immediately*.

3. Conversation (Philippians 1:27; 1 Timothy 4:12; Hebrews 13:5). Meant *behavior* or *manner of life*. A really colloquial version could render it "life-style." For numerous examples of the use of this word and the effect it can have on exegesis, consult a concordance.

4. Let (Isaiah 43:13; 2 Thessalonians 2:7). The original languages carried the idea of *restrain* or *hinder*, and this is what the English word "let" meant in 1611. Today it means "to allow." Thus correct exegesis of passages containing it can be difficult for English readers.

5. Prevent (Psalms 21:3; 119:147; 1 Thessalonians 4:15). In 1611 it meant "precede," and so correctly translated the originals. Today it means to stop or ban.

6. Quick (Ephesians 2:1 Hebrews 4:12; 1 Peter 3:16; 4:5). Meant *alive*, not *speedy*.

These are only a few of the most obvious examples.

In addition to these reasons, which had become obvious to the average intelligent reader, scholars were aware of at least two others. For one thing, since 1611, numerous Greek manuscripts of the New Testament or parts of it have been discovered, including the two great finds of Tischendorf—Vaticanus and Sinaiticus. These have resulted in some revisions of the Greek text to bring it closer to the original.[4] Then, too, continued studies of the Greek and Hebrew languages and discoveries of ancient documents, letters, and other everyday communications in the languages have added much to our knowledge of what the original words meant to the common people, and thus shed light on their usage by the writers.

Another century of revision begins. Scholars did not suddenly become aware of these facts at the beginning of the twentieth century. They had been a growing concern. As early as 1755 John Wesley recognized three areas in which the King James Version could be improved: "better text, better sense, better English."[5] Scholar that he was, he produced an excellent New Testament translation which, however, never achieved widespread notice.

In 1904, the wife of a Congregational minister, recognizing that the children in her Bible classes were "not making head nor tail" out of the Scriptures she encouraged them to read, became responsible for a popular translation known as the *Twentieth Century New Testament.* It was produced by a number of laymen with an interest in Greek and was good enough that Moody Bible Institute republished it and has kept it in print.

Since then numerous individuals with a knowledge of Greek have produced New Testaments that achieved varying degrees of quality and popularity. A few of the more familiar names are Weymouth, Moffatt, Goodspeed, Beck, Williams, Phillips, Wuest and Taylor.

The first modern committee for translation met in response to a call of the Convocation of Canterbury, England, issued in 1870. Although American scholars were originally associated with it, there was sufficient divergence in viewpoint between the British and Americans that eventually two versions grew out of it: the English Revision (N.T. 1881, O.T. 1884), and the *American Standard Version* of 1901.

The *American Standard Version* has been described as the best Greek and worst English version ever published. It is so literal that Greek students use it as a pony for their translation assignments. Yet the attempt to be literal was done so slavishly as to result in a wooden English. As a study Bible it is invaluable; for devotional and public reading it is scarcely worthy the grandeur of its theme. The *New American Standard Bible* is an effort to revise the *American Standard Version* with a view to correcting these weaknesses and producing an equally excellent study Bible expressed in more pleasing English. Among conservatives, this version has come to rank in popularity next to the King James.

The three most recent committee versions—all produced within the third quarter of this century—are: the *Revised Standard Version* (RSV) which was planned to replace the *American Standard Version* as the time approached for the latter's copyright to expire; the *New English Bible* (NEB), intended to appeal to the unchurched. Its English is beautiful and a delight to read, but this effect is achieved by translations so free as to border at times of paraphrase. The *New International Version* (NIV) is a work done entirely by evangelical scholars. It has achieved a happy balance of literalness and good English, and shows evidence of becoming widely accepted in conservative circles.

How Can I, A Mere Layman, Decide What Version to Use?

The above discussion has probably raised some questions. The first may be: What did you mean by branding a version as "slavishly" literal? Anyone with even a little high school language knows there is not a one-to-one correspondence between the vocabulary of one language and that of another. Most words have a range of meaning, and the translator must select the one that seems to best fit the context and intent of the writer. This involves even the most conscientious translator in the realm of interpretation, and ultimately his decision may depend on what theological position he already holds. Thus, other things being equal, a translation by conservatives is usually more reliable than one by liberals, no matter how efficient the latter may be in the study of the language. For example, the *New World Translation*, put out by Jehovah's Witnesses, goes out of its way to eliminate any rendering that implies the deity of Christ, even if the normal Greek has to be forced or revised to bolster their rejection of this doctrine.

Not only may the slavishly literal translation seek a one-to-one correspondence of words, it also tends to ignore the idiom of a language; that is, the conventional idiosyncracies of expression. This is an outgrowth of word-for-word transliteration that may result in a very awkward rendering, or even in the real meaning being lost. A simple example from elementary French would be the reply of someone asked his age. In his own tongue a French child would literally say, "I have ten years." But he should translate into English as "I am ten years old," in order to be both accurate and idiomatic. Or, perhaps you can imagine the difficulty this writer once had trying to explain to a Spanish friend what he meant by saying, "I am taking a busman's holiday."

To give a Bible example, we tend to speak of anything which involves our deepest emotions as coming from our hearts, and when we use the expression we are understood very well. The ancients, however, conceived of the intestinal area as being the seat of their emotions and affections. Therefore, when their expressions of deeply held feelings were taken over into the nearest English equivalents, the result was such expressions as "bowels of mercies"[6] and "the bowels of the saints are refreshed by thee"[7] which strike the English ear as puzzling vulgarities. It is more accurate in the light of the idiomatic meaning of the original writer to change the word in translation to "heart," as many modern versions do.

A second question might be, What is the difference between a translation and a paraphrase? The simplest answer is that a translation keeps as close as possible to the words of the original without becoming so slavish that it makes nonsense in English. A paraphraser, on the other hand, puts into his own words or the words of the people he hopes to reach, what

Which Version Should I Use?

appears to him to be the essential meaning of the original. In this sense a paraphrase has more in common with a commentary than with a translation. It is thus only as reliable as is the insight and theological understanding of the paraphraser. No matter how conservative such a man might be, his Bible should not be one's major contact with God's Word, or the basis of serious Bible study. A good paraphrase, however, may be helpful for devotional reading and for shedding new light on old familiar passages. Among evangelicals, the two most popular paraphrases are J. B. Phillips, *The New Testament in Modern English*, and Kenneth Taylor, *The Living Bible*.

Sometimes there is a fine line between a translation and a paraphrase, as in the case of the *New English Bible*. Like Moffatt, this version even rearranges the order of verses in some Old Testament passages.

Good News for Modern Man (TEV) is another which falls into the borderline category. It was conceived as a translation limited to using common English words that would be understood by those to whom English is a second language, but it immediately became overwhelmingly popular with college students and with others who had never been comfortable with the Elizabethan tongue. In its efforts to simplify, however, this version has sometimes crossed over the line into a paraphrase. A more serious complaint, however, is that the translator's theological bias frequently comes through. He admittedly does not accept the deity of Christ.

Obviously a layman who knows only English is not in a position to judge how faithful a translation is to the original. There are, however, a few texts that conservative reviewers turn to in evaluating a new translation. Among these are the "virgin" passages. Translators who substitute "young woman" or something similar, may be suspected of bowing to liberal theological bias.

In Psalm 2:12, the phrase "Kiss the Son" has been rendered by some as "Kiss his feet." This requires taking some liberties with the text and suggests a deliberate effort to play down the Messianic aspect of the Psalm.

Another illustration of playing down the Messianic element is found in Psalm 45:6 where, "Thy throne, O God, is for ever and ever" becomes in the *Revised Standard Version*, "Your divine throne endures for ever," and in the *New English Bible*, "Your throne is like God's throne, eternal."

The famous "I know that my redeemer liveth" of Job 19:25, becomes in the *New English Bible*, "I know that my vindicator lives and that he will rise last to speak in court."

The choice of a translation must also depend on the purpose of the user. The Revised Scofield, which uses the King James text but modernizes the archaic words, is not difficult to understand and still has the stately grace suitable for public reading of God's Word.

For a study Bible for private use, though not for public reading, the *New American Standard Bible* receives the commendation of most conservative scholars. The *New International Version* bids fair to win equal acceptance and many think is better suited for public reading.

Finally, it must be emphasized that no one translation is better or worse than the others in every verse. That which excels in one passage may be quite awkward or misleading in another. The miracle is that in every recognized version, even those which have been most highly criticized, the Word of God comes through in power, converting sinners and changing lives. Through all its handling and even mishandling by men of many degrees of intellect, piety and theological persuasion, it still proves itself to be "quick (i.e., living) and powerful, and sharper than any two-edged sword"[8]—in fact, the inspired, inerrant, eternal and life-giving Word of the living God. This has been well expressed in the testimony of one scholar who served on the translation committee of the *New International Version*:

> I discovered that there was a richness of meaning to be found in reading the many helpful translations that have appeared in this century. No single translation that has come out in print

Which Version Should I Use?

gives the best rendering of every verse. For various passages in the New Testament one will find the clearest and richest rendering in Weymouth or Goodspeed, in Berkeley or Beck, in the NASB or ACT. Paul says: "That ye . . . may be able to comprehend with all saints what is the breadth and length, and depth, and height" (Ephesians 3:18). Different translators get varying insights into the meaning of particular passages. The student of the Bible will go deeper and higher, wider and further in his understanding of the Word as he uses different translations.[9]

SUMMARY

The wealth of English translations of the Bible that have appeared in this century are evidence of the difficulty of even the finest scholars to produce a "best" version. These translations range all the way from the slavishly literal to the paraphrase. All reflect in some manner the theological stance of the translator.

If a choice must be made, good theology is to be preferred over beautiful English; a literal translation over a paraphrase. However, the serious student or devotional reader will try to have available several of the better versions for the sake of finding deeper insights into the wealth of meaning to be gained from God's living Word.

FOOTNOTES

[1] Quoted in *The New Testament from 26 Translations* (Grand Rapids: Zondervan Publishing House, 1967), Introduction.

[2] One important change between the Old and New Scofield relates to Bishop Ussher's dates which were introduced into the margin of King James Bibles in 1701. They are based on the assumption that the genealogies can be a valid basis for chronology. The revisers of the New Scofield have removed those dates and substituted their own chronology based on modern methods of historical research.

[3] Hab. 2:2

[4] See discussion in chapter 8

[5] The New Testament translated by John Wesley, John C. Winston Edition, 1938. Introduction, p. x.

[6] Col. 3:12

[7] Philem. 7

[8] Heb. 4:12

[9] Ralph Earle, *How We Got Our Bible*, p. 118f

Chapter 11

How Can I Get More Out Of Bible Study?

God intended His revelation to be understood. Revelation means "that which is revealed," or, "disclosing to others that which was before unknown to them." David said that God's Word was "a lamp unto my feet, and a light unto my path."[1] Lights are used to make a path plainer, not to obscure it. The Lord ordered Habakkuk to "Write the vision, and make it plain."[2] Jesus said, "Ye shall know the truth,"[3] and John said that he wrote in order "that ye might believe."[4]

Higher education, therefore, is not required in order to understand the Word of God. While there are many buried treasures that may be profitably mined and brought to light by those who are proficient in languages and history, the Holy Spirit has carefully scattered the precious jewels of salvation and obedient living where all who will may gather them. The most poorly educated saint whose mind is yielded to the tutoring of the Holy Spirit is a better Bible student than is a Doctor of Philosophy who studies it through the blinders of self-sufficiency and scientific materialism. An often quoted statement of Dr. William Lyons Phelps, one time President of Yale University, underscores this truth: "I believe a knowledge of the Bible without a college course is more valuable than a college course without the Bible."

How Shall I Approach It?

A major reason for the errors that warped the medieval church was the fact that God's Word was kept from the common people. They were taught that they could not possibly understand it and that it must be interpreted to them through the media of the specially educated priests. Wherever the direct light of Scripture did reach men, understanding was apparent. Studies of isolated Christian groups who had the Scripture shows us that even though they were unrelated to one another in time or geography, their doctrine and behavior were remarkably similar to each other. When the Bible is allowed to speak for itself, it speaks plainly.

This should not surprise us since we are told that the Holy Spirit is the real Teacher of the Book He authored.[5] The Word, therefore, is rightly approached in a spirit of submission to His direction. It is as James I. Packer has said, "God's Book does not yield up its secrets to those who will not be taught of the Spirit."[6]

With these things in mind, even the most timid student willing to be taught of the Holy Spirit can approach Bible study with confidence and expectation.

What to avoid. Expecting the Bible to speak plainly rules out two common but misguided approaches. The first is *eisegetical*—searching the Scripture for proof texts to uphold a doctrine or practice that we are already determined to accept. The preconceived viewpoint we are trying to bolster may or may not be the Scriptural one—that is not the issue here—but we will never really know until we submit it to the light of God's Word and as conscientiously examine those passages that appear to contradict it as we do those which appear to uphold it.

The second mistaken approach is the allegorical or spiritualizing method. It was popularized by St. Augustine in his *City of God* when he applied the millennial prophecies to the Rome of Constantine because it had wedded itself to the church. In time, allegory became the normal medieval method of interpretation, with the plain literal meaning buried under explanations that became more and more fanciful.

To say this is not to ignore the fact that the Bible, and especially the Old Testament, is filled with people, objects, and events that typify or illustrate the purpose and ministry of the Messiah and the life of the church. The Book of Hebrews explains how the tabernacle illustrated Christ and His ministry. But the tabernacle was also a real tent with real furnishings that the Israelites carried about with them on their journeyings. The brazen serpent, on the warrant of our Lord Himself[7] was an illustration of the efficacy of His crucifixion. But first it was a literal, visible, touchable object of bronze that did a work of healing in the nation. So graphic was the memory of its efficacy that in later generations it became an idol and had to be destroyed.[8] And Paul tells us in 1 Corinthians 10 that the events of the history of Israel furnish types or examples applicable to our daily walk in this world. He illustrates with references to events in the books of Exodus and Numbers, but he carefully states "these things happened to them"—they were literal historical events experienced by literal historical people.

In the New Testament allegorizing has been popular for handling the parables of Jesus. And while it may sometimes produce helpful applications, as a primary approach to Bible study its effect is to obscure and even warp the basic intent of a passage.

What should I look for? The proper approach to the Scripture is to take it at face value; that is, what it says in normal language. Recognize that the prophets were ordinary people speaking to ordinary people as the Spirit directed them. This is the *exegetical* approach. Instead of hoping to read into the Word of God what we want to find there, we seek to find and draw out of it what God has actually said. Nor are we to seek first for a fanciful explanation, but to ascertain the literal or normal meaning of what is being said. When the Bible says that a great fish swallowed Jonah it is saying that a real man in a real time and place was swallowed whole by a real fish. Now, Jesus did say that fish was a picture of the grave where He would lie for three days, but He prefaced it by saying, "As Jonah was three days and three nights in the whale's belly."[9] So, if Jonah's experience did not really happen, we could question whether Jesus meant to convey that the resurrection would be a literal happening.

Of course we recognize the Bible contains idioms and figures of speech. How many tons of paper have been wasted in arguing whether the Bible contains an error when it has Joshua say, "Sun, stand thou still . . . " when even now with our knowledge of the rotation of the earth, we still say "the sun rose," and "the sun set." When Jesus said, "Ye are the salt of the earth,"[10] He obviously did not mean we are white crystals to be poured from a shaker. Neither, however, did He mean nothing literally understandable by it. He is saying that if we meditate on the literal properties of salt we will understand better how He expects us to live on earth. Hell may or may not be a literal fire, but if it is not, it is something unfamiliar to us on earth of which fire is the most closely related element we can understand.

With these cautions in mind, we may approach Bible study asking three questions of any given passage. The first is, what does it say? When we read that Eve ate the fruit of a forbidden tree, we are supposed to understand Eve took a real piece of fruit from a real tree and took a real bite out of it. We have no warrant for saying that her sin was to engage in sexual intercourse, as some like to suggest. A corollary to this is to avoid letting it say what it does not say. Scripture nowhere tells us the fruit was an apple.

To know what the Bible really says, we need to know the context of a passage. As one preacher said, "A text without its context is a pretext." For instance, an atheist might get away with telling someone ignorant of the Scripture that the Bible says, "There is no God." But if the person bothers to look it up he will discover that, while the words are actually there, the

How Can I Get More Out Of Bible Study?

statement in context says, "The fool hath said in his heart, there is no God."[11] One of the ways in which Satan sought to tempt our Lord involved taking Scripture out of context.[12] He still uses that method.

Again, reams of explanation have been wasted on the question, "Where did Cain get his wife?" because superficial readers have looked at the opening verses of Genesis 4 and concluded, "The Bible says there was one original couple and they had two boys, so how did the human race come from them?" If they had only read a little further into the beginning of chapter 5, they would have discovered that, during a long life of nine hundred and thirty years, Adam "begat sons and daughters."

After ascertaining what a passage says, our next question is, What does it mean? One of the most controversial of our Lord's parables states that the kingdom of heaven is like a woman who hid leaven in a batch of dough. No one who has ever made bread or seen it made has the least difficulty understanding what He is saying, but what He meant by it has been the subject of endless controversy. Is the leaven a picture of the gospel that will enable the church to expand endlessly, or is it a picture of Satan's evil wiles by which the church will experience an unnatural growth at the cost of its original purity? A good way to decide this question is to study every passage of Scripture where leaven is mentioned. By using a concordance they can readily be found. God's Word is consistent in its use of symbols, for His purpose is to enlighten us, not to confuse us.

Jesus gave us a most important clue to ascertaining the meaning of Scripture when He said, "they are they which testify of Me,"[13] and when on the road to Emmaus He expounded "in all the Scriptures the things concerning Himself." The Bible is essentially one Book with one theme and message which the ancient fish symbol of the church states succinctly—Jesus Christ, Son of God, Saviour. Or, as St. Augustine put it, "The New is in the Old concealed; the Old is in the New revealed."

Any study of Scripture that does not bring us closer in understanding and appreciation of the Person and work of our Saviour has failed in its essential purpose.

The final question to ask is, What does this mean to me? This question refers to *application*, of which there may be many as the Holy Spirit uses the Word to meet a specific need of a person in his individual situation. While a passage may justly have only one interpretation, it may have many applications. Unfortunately, too many people start and end their Bible study with this question. Their only interest is to have a quick and easy answer for today's difficulty. At its lowest, this attitude leads to the "magic" practice of seeking guidance by letting the pages fall open at random and acting on the first words one sees. It is true that the Holy Spirit often brings to bear some llumination from the Word of God on the present situation of one of His children, but those who consistently find the greatest comfort and the clearest and most constant guidance from the Scripture are those who become people of the Book by making themselves familiar with what it says and what it means.

In addition, it must be said that those who best discover both meaning and application in the Bible are those who approach it with the intent of submitting themselves to whatever it teaches them, both as to what they must believe and how they must behave. The Holy Spirit does not yield up the treasures of Scripture for the purpose of inflating our intellects and egos, but for the purpose of securing our wills. "If any man will do his will, he shall know of the doctrine," Jesus said.[15] And through James the Spirit commanded, "Be ye doers of the Word, and not hearers only."[16]

Where Shall I Start?

Studying the Bible involves much more than reading ten verses a day (often unrelated to those of the day before and the day after) along with a devotional commentary. While this is a good step of personal devotion, it does not provide one with a basic knowledge of the content and interpretation of Scripture.

How Can I Get More Out Of Bible Study?

When one has made up his mind to conscientiously and consistently study God's Word, the first question with which he is confronted is, "Where shall I begin?"

Two basic methods. Courses on "How to Study the Bible" often include a section on "Types of Bible Study" with a long list of sub-headings. Basically, however, there are two major approaches. One is topical. This would include the study of a given doctrine or character or word (love, leaven, hell, priest, etc.) or subject. It includes such popular type series as all the animals, trees, rivers, mountains, or children in the Bible. It is a popular method in that one can rather quickly collate all the references to the chosen topic by use of a concordance or topical Bible, learn what is said about it, and make useful applications. It provides a sense of accomplishment in the immediate awareness of having acquired a worthwhile body of Scriptural knowledge on the given subject. Chapter 2, on what the Bible has to say about itself, is an example of this approach.

The other basic approach is the book study. This includes survey studies of the Bible as a whole, or of one of the Testaments as a whole in order to grasp the overall history and development of its message, and to provide a framework into which people and events and other details can be placed.

The value of studying an individual book of the Bible in depth is that we are taking a God-given unit of Scripture as a manageable portion for our study. In such a study we learn what God had to say through a specific individual to a given audience at a particular situation in time. Beyond this lies the universal message to analogous people and times. Where the writer refers to a problem, his understanding of that matter can be related to his message as a whole and can then be accurately and usefully incorporated into a larger study. His book or message should also be seen in the light of his position in the whole Scripture and his place in the development of God's full revelation. Part of the study of an Old Testament book should also include whatever light the New Testament throws on it by specific references. Genesis, for instance, should include study of New Testament references to the days of Noah, the faith of Abraham, the destruction of Sodom, the profanity of Esau—to mention just a few.

A New Testament book would include study of the context of any Old Testament allusions. For example, wherever in Matthew we read "that it might be fulfilled which was spoken by the prophet," we should find and study the message originally given. The use of marginal notes or of a concordance facilitates the finding of such cross references. Some Old Testament and New Testament books might very well be studied in parallel; for example; Leviticus and Hebrews, Numbers and Ephesians, Daniel and Revelation.

Any book study should begin with reading the book through at a sitting, preferably more than once, and with an attempt to find its key verse. (Harry Ironside used to say the key was usually pretty close to the front or back door.) G. Campbell Morgan is supposed to have stated that he never attempted to write an exposition of a book until he had read it through at least fifty times.

Once the basic content of the book as a whole has been grasped, it can be outlined and broken down into sections, chapters, verses, and even words, for in-depth study. To begin with the larger unit and work to the smaller is a valuable rule of thumb. It leaves one less vulnerable to the error of misinterpreting a statement because it has been taken apart from its context.

Tools. Every workman has tools suitable to his trade and, let us make no mistake about it, study is work. Bible study is hard work because it requires us to handle the most important subject on earth, but by the same token it is the most satisfying, yes, the most joyous, work one can undertake.

Like any other work, Bible study has its tools and the committed student will gradually acquire a full chest of them. We have already mentioned a concordance, which is basic. Without it the effort of finding related passages or all the references to a particular subject would be time consuming and

How Can I Get More Out of Bible Study?

probably incomplete. A topical Bible is also very helpful in this respect.

A good Bible dictionary is probably the next most important item. This is a ready reference for acquiring background information on any person, place, object or other word mentioned in Scripture.

It is helpful to have several standard translations of the Bible. Seeing different ways in which a single word can be translated is often helpful in understanding its meaning. *The New Testament from 26 Translations* is excellent for this purpose. There are also several parallel-column translations on the market. If you can read a foreign language by all means use a Bible in that translation also. Seeing how another language translates a word can furnish much insight.

A good illustration of this concerns the expression "earnest of the Spirit" in 2 Corinthians 1:22 and Ephesians 1:14. The Spanish word used for "earnest" is *arras*. An *arras* is the name given a small coin which at a certain point in the wedding ceremony a Spanish bridegroom folds into the palm of his bride to symbolize the fact that he is now taking responsibility for the supply of her needs. Is that not a beautiful illustration of what the verse is saying?

In addition to these basic tools, there is much helpful material in the way of handbooks, atlases and commentaries. Commentaries, however, should be selected with care and they should never, never become a substitute for personal Bible study. If they are consulted *after* you have thoroughly studied a passage and obtained a message and application from it yourself, it may give additional helpful insights, and perhaps correct a limited understanding. More than that, it is quite likely to give you a major boost of self-confidence that encourages you to further study when you discover that what you have yourself gleaned from the passage is what the commentator is presenting. An atlas is valuable for increasing your understanding of the geographical settings of scriptural events.

Finally, a notebook or other good means of preserving the

results of your study is indispensable. You can include with it the notes you have taken from speakers and teachers. As you see your material growing and demanding more space, you will have concrete evidence of your accomplishment as well as courage to continue.

A woman once said, "I don't need to study the Bible any more. I know everything in it from Sunday school." She was wrong. You will never complete your study of the Bible. It yields immediate rewards to the newest babe in Christ, but Bible knowledge builds on itself, constantly yielding new surprises and treasures. Those who have worked at it the longest and delved the deepest testify that they have scarcely reached below the surface, but are constantly discovering new treasures.

SUMMARY

Effective Bible study is to be approached with an open and humble mind in order to learn what it teaches and not necessarily what we want it to teach. Its purpose is not *eisegesis*, reading into it what we hope to find, but *exegesis*, getting out of it what the Holy Spirit has put there.

The two major types of approach to the Bible are topical studies and book studies. These have many sub-types.

Every passage of Scripture should be approached with three questions in this order: What does it say? What does it mean? How shall I apply it?

The Bible itself should be the focus of our attention, but there are certain helpful tools that will make the task more efficient or clarify difficulties. Next to an assortment of translations, the most useful are a concordance, a Bible dictionary and an atlas.

Bible study is an expanding task and joy. One never fully plumbs its depths.

FOOTNOTES

[1] Psa. 119:105
[2] Heb. 2:2
[3] John 8:32
[4] John 20:31
[5] 1 Cor. 2:14
[6] *Fundamentalism and the Word of God.* Grand Rapids: Wm. B. Eerdman Publishing Co., 1958, p. 112.
[7] John 3:14
[8] 2 Kings 18:4
[9] Matt. 12:40
[10] Matt. 5:13
[11] Psa. 14:1; 53:1
[12] Matt. 4:6; cf. Psa. 91:11-12
[13] John 5:39
[14] Luke 24:27; see also vs. 44
[15] John 7:17
[16] James 1:22

Chapter 12

What Is My Responsibility To An Infallible Bible?

We have sought to demonstrate that the Bible we possess is indeed the Word of God, inspired and infallible, and faithfully transmitted to us. We should not fail to note, however, that the ultimate assurance that God has spoken is the fact of the resurrection of Christ. In that act God placed His approval on all that Jesus said and did, and He said over and over, "It is written," thereby accepting and quoting the Old Testament of God's Word. Furthermore, He promised His apostles the Holy Spirit who would speak of Him and guide them into all truth.[1]

There remains yet one important question to be asked: "What obligation does the possession of such a Book place on me?" Here again, the Scripture itself is our best source for an answer.

Every privilege in life carries with it commensurate responsibilities. In a society where everyone is constantly screaming for his rights we tend to forget this. Nevertheless, it is a basic element in God's moral order. Certainly no privilege can be greater than that of having God's infallible revelation. The responsibility that accompanies it is apparent from the very beginning when Moses completed writing the Torah and ordered it placed beside the ark of the covenant "that it may be there for a witness against thee."[2] In other words, from that day on, the life of God's people would be judged by the standard of the Book.

On the understanding, then, that this Book will ultimately

be our judge, it makes three demands on us that we dare not ignore. One of the best examples of a person who understood and acted on these demands was Ezra, whose commitment has been mentioned previously. The Scripture describes him as one who "prepared his heart to seek the law of the Lord, and to do it, and to teach in Israel statutes and judgments."[3] We will, therefore, discuss our responsibility to the Book under the three areas of knowing it, doing it, and teaching it.

Know It

A book merely residing beside the ark in the Holy of Holies would be of no real benefit to the people of God. It was intended to be known. Thus were the Levites charged with the special duty of making it known. Whenever Israel's leaders sought revival, they began by making the Scripture more widely known. A good example of this is the action of King Jehoshaphat who organized a teaching mission throughout his whole realm.[4]

Rulers were given a special responsibility in this matter. No matter what other ability and preparation their position required, it was of first importance that they be immersed in the truths of God's Word. Joshua, the first leader to whom the written Word was available, was told that his success would depend on his meditating in it day and night.[5] In Deuteronomy there are instructions governing the behavior of any future king. They include the requirement that when he came to the throne he should write out for himself a copy of the Torah from the copy that was before the priests and Levites, and then should read it continually for the rest of his days "that he may learn to fear the Lord his God, to keep all the words of this law and these statutes, to do them: That his heart be not lifted up above his brethren, and that he turn not aside from the commandment, to the right hand, or to the left; to the end that he may prolong his days in his kingdom, he, and his children, in the midst of Israel."[6]

Studied in the light of this command, the history of the

What Is My Responsibility To An Infallible Bible?

kingdom shows that the deterioration in character of the kings is directly related to their neglect of God's Word. Every revival began with a rediscovery of the knowledge of what God had revealed. Hezekiah, Josiah and Ezra are good examples of this.[7] The story of Hezekiah's revival covers three chapters in 2 Chronicles, from 29 through 31. It is an interesting exercise to go through them and notice how frequently he refers to the law of Moses (or of the Lord) and the Psalms of David as the authority for his actions.

David, the man after God's heart, was the king who most literally and seriously followed the injunction of Deuteronomy 17. His psalms are filled with expressions of his love for God's Word and the blessings it brought to him. Almost every one of the 176 verses of Psalm 119 has something significant to say about God's Word and what it meant to him. In it he uses eight synonyms in attempting to describe it. You can find them all in the first two cantos. And, remember, David had only a very small portion of our Old Testament, probably eight or nine books at most.

In charging his son Solomon with the responsibilities of the succession, this necessity of clinging to God's Word was the focus of his emphasis. David commanded Solomon to "keep the charge of the Lord thy God, to walk in his ways, to keep his statutes, and his commandments, and his judgments, and his testimonies, as it is written in the law of Moses, that thou mayest prosper in all thou doest."[8] How reminiscent that is of Jehovah's charge to Joshua. Tragically, Solomon grew lax in this primary responsibility and soon failed to live up to the promise of his early days.

The heart of Paul the apostle was burdened for the spread of the knowledge of Scripture in the young churches. It is the burden of his last letter where it is stressed over and over to Timothy the importance of knowing the Word and making it known. To this devout young man who had been familiar with the Scripture from earliest childhood, he commands in the words of one of the most memorized of all verses: "Study to show thyself approved unto God, a workman that needeth not to be ashamed, rightly dividing the word of truth."[9]

Showing that he practiced what he preached, the aged apostle who himself had known the Scriptures from boyhood and who now languished in a Roman dungeon facing imminent death, begged his young pupil to visit him and bring him his "books, but especially the parchments."[10]

Nor must we overlook the fact that before Ezra could seek to know God's Word, he "prepared his heart." He needed a prepared heart for his task. The Lord does not reveal His treasures to those who seek mere intellectual satisfaction or self-glory, but to those who are prepared to submit to it, willingly to be judged by it, and ready to acknowledge their responsibility to it.

Do It

There was once a missionary who encouraged his converts to memorize the Scripture. He was very much pleased when one man, whom he had considered rather slow, came to his home one night and recited a number of verses perfectly. "How did you ever do it so well?" he exclaimed admiringly.

"Well," explained the convert, "it was awfully hard at first, but then I figured out a way. I would read over one verse and then I would practice doing what it said for a while. After that, remembering it would be easy and I would go on to the next verse."

This man had caught the spirit of Ezra who sought not only to know the Word, but to do it, and the intent of James who commanded, "Be ye doers of the word and not hearers only."[11]

Of course, the first thing we must "do" when we are confronted with God's Word is to allow it to judge us. When we agree with its judgment that we are sinners, only then can we accept the gift of salvation that God promises us through its pages. No amount of "doing" will ever earn salvation for us. The Scripture makes that abundantly clear.[12] But once we have received the gift, it is equally clear that our responsibility is to become doers of the Word, for the verse that immediately follows the assurance that eternal life is a gift, goes on to explain that we are "created in Christ Jesus (that is, made new creatures as 2 Corinthians 5:17 expresses it) unto good works."[13]

Doing the Word is a responsibility, but not a burden. "If ye love me, keep my commandments," Jesus said.[14] It is a responsibility called forth by our love and our gratitude, and no one has ever felt burdened while doing the deeds by which he says, "I love you." A homely illustration of this is found in the old story of the little girl who was asked if the baby she was carrying was not much too heavy for her. "Of course he isn't," she retorted. "He's my brother."

Doing God's Word is the only concrete way we have of saying "I love you" to the Saviour.

Teach it

The goal of Ezra's life went even beyond knowing and doing the Word of God. The desire of his heart was to teach it to others. This, too, is to be the culmination of a Christian's knowing and doing. "Go . . . and teach," the Lord commanded His disciples.[15] Paul instructed Timothy to commit (or teach) to faithful men all that he had learned in order that they should "be able to teach others also."[16]

Lest you say, "Yes, but that is for the pastor or Sunday school teacher, but I couldn't teach," there are further passages to look at. It is true that the Holy Spirit gives to some a special gift for teaching,[17] but He has also made it clear that teaching others (not necessarily formally) is the responsibility of every Christian. Do you remember what happened when the first church of Jerusalem was hit by severe persecution so that the members had to flee for their lives? Acts 8:4 tells us "they that were scattered abroad went everywhere preaching the word." But if you look up to verse 1 you will see that those who fled did not include the apostles—the official teachers. They remained in Jerusalem. It was the ordinary laymen who taught the new faith wherever they went. Remember, too, how the author of Hebrews scolded his hearers because they still needed to be fed like babies even though they had been Christian hearers long enough to have reached "the time ye ought to be teachers."[18]

Recognizing then that we each ought to be teachers, an important question is, "Who shall I teach?" Again, the Scripture has the answer.

To your family. It seems always to have been the Lord's plan that the basic schoolroom should be the home. He instructed Israel that God's laws should be the constant topic of their conversation in the home.[19] That law included the command "Honor thy father and thy mother."[20] Surely one of the reasons behind this command was to ease the teaching task, for an important way in which a child honors his parents is to heed and obey their teaching.

The Lord even put planned object lessons into the hands of his teacher-parents. One of these was the annual Feast of the Passover which gave parents the opportunity to explain how the Lord had redeemed them out of slavery in Egypt.[21] To this day, the youngest child in a Jewish home is expected to memorize four questions and ask them at the family table during the Passover celebration. They begin: "Why is this night different from all other nights?" It is the father's cue to launch into a long historical recital which begins, "We were Pharaoh's slaves and the Lord our God led us out with a mighty hand..."

Again, when Joshua led the nation across the Jordan River into the Promised Land, he ordered the priests to build a memorial out of the stones in the river bed so they could describe God's faithfulness in keeping His promise to Abraham when in time to come their children would ask, "What mean ye by these stones?"[22]

A mother of twelve children went to her pastor to say she thought she had been called to preach. The pastor agreed with her, but added, "And the Lord has even supplied you with a congregation of twelve." It was in such a classroom that John Wesley had his first lessons in biblical theology, for his mother made it her chief aim to see that each of her eighteen children

What Is My Responsibility To An Infallible Bible?

had at least one hour a week of uninterrupted personal teaching time with her. And Timothy, whom we have had occasion to mention so frequently, knew the Scriptures from a child because his mother and grandmother had been his teachers.[23]

David even wrote a psalm about the importance of teaching the truths of God and His mighty works to each coming generation.[24] The Scriptures plainly require us to be teachers at home.

To your community. It is said that Hannah Wesley's teaching did not stop with her children, but that her parlor was known as a place where neighbors often came in to hear the Bible expounded.

It was the communities to which the persecuted Christians from Jerusalem fled that benefitted by their teaching.[25] And surely when the writer of Hebrews said that his hearers had reached the time when they ought to be teachers, he was thinking of their responsibility to expound their faith to those whom their lives touched.

Teaching our community may mean taking a Sunday school class, or helping in a youth organization, or opening our homes to a child evangelism class or a Bible study group. It will always mean, in the words of Peter, "being ready always to give an answer to every man that asketh you a reason of the hope that is in you."[26]

To your world. Our teaching responsibility is not complete unless it goes far beyond our own homes and communities. "Teach all nations" were the last words of our Lord before His ascension.[27] Nor are we free to say that this command is not also our responsibility. No one person can literally go and teach "all nations." Even the foreign missionary has his limited sphere of direct service. Each of us has a share in the teaching of all nations as we recognize our responsibility to do so, to seek the way the Lord would have us discharge it, and to make the work of others possible by our prayers and material support. This is not a cop-out unless one uses it to evade the direct call of God; it is a necessary element in the task of teaching all nations.

Nor should we overlook the fact that all nations have found their way to our own doorsteps as the flower of their youth has flocked to our universities, hospitals and even business establishments, and countless thousands of refugees have stormed our shorelines. Right at home we have been given the opportunity to obey the command to teach all nations.

Finally, it should be noted that whatever we do to fulfill the task of teaching all nations becomes an object lesson and teaching tool to those in our own families as they question the meaning of our activities or prayers or gifts. And so our teaching comes full circle. Who knows but what, because of our commitments, they may hear the call and catch the vision literally to go and teach all nations.

Knowing that our Bible is God's inspired and inerrant and faithfully preserved revelation is of little value to us unless we commit ourselves anew to our responsibility of knowing it, doing it, and teaching it.

SUMMARY

Because God has given us His inerrant revelation, by which also He will judge us, we are responsible to order our lives by it. Succinctly, this means we are to know it—which means study, to do or obey it, and to teach it either formally or informally as the Lord leads us in our families, our communities, and our world. This is the expected fruit of an infallible Bible. God's Word does not return unto Him void.[28]

FOOTNOTES

[1] John 14:26; 16:13
[2] Deut. 31:26
[3] Ezra 7:10
[4] 2 Chron. 17:7-9
[5] Josh. 1:8
[6] Deut. 17:18-20
[7] 2 Kings 18:6; 2 Chron. 31:21; 34:14-21, 29-33; Neh. 8:1-18

[8] 1 Kings 2:3
[9] 2 Tim. 2:15
[10] 2 Tim. 4:13
[11] James 1:22
[12] Eph. 2:8-9
[13] Eph. 2:10
[14] John 14:15
[15] Matt. 28:19
[16] 2 Tim. 2:2
[17] Eph. 4:11
[18] Heb. 5:12
[19] Deut. 6:7
[20] Deut. 5:16
[21] Exod. 12:26-27; 13:8, 14-16; Deut. 6:20-25
[22] Joshua 4:6-7, 21-24
[23] 2 Tim. 1:5; 3:15
[24] Psa. 78:1-8
[25] Acts 8:4; 11:19-21
[26] 1 Peter 3:15
[27] Matt. 28:19-20
[28] Isa. 55:11